# Bichons Frises

**ELAINE WALDORF GEWIRTZ**

*Bichons Frises*
Project Team
Editor: Stephanie Fornino
Copy Editor: Joann Woy
Indexer: Lucie Haskins
Interior Design: Leah Lococo Ltd. and Stephanie Krautheim
Design Layout: Angela Stanford

T.F.H. Publications
President/CEO: Glen S. Axelrod
Executive Vice President: Mark E. Johnson
Publisher: Christopher T. Reggio
Production Manager: Kathy Bontz

T.F.H. Publications, Inc.
One TFH Plaza
Third and Union Avenues
Neptune City, NJ 07753

*Discovery Communications, Inc. Book
Development Team:*
Marjorie Kaplan, President, Animal Planet Media
Carol LeBlanc, Vice President, Licensing
Elizabeth Bakacs, Vice President, Creative Services
Brigid Ferraro, Director, Licensing
Peggy Ang, Director, Animal Planet Marketing
Caitlin Erb, Licensing Specialist

Printed and bound in China
08 09 10 11 12 1 3 5 7 9 8 6 4 2

**Library of Congress Cataloging-in-Publication Data**
Gewirtz, Elaine Waldorf.
  Bichons frises / Elaine Waldorf Gewirtz.
      p. cm. – (Animal planet pet care library)
  Includes index.
  ISBN 978-0-7938-3788-5 (alk. paper)
  1. Bichon frise. I. Title.
SF429.B52G49 2008
636.72–dc22
                                    2007029602

This book has been published with the intent to provide accurate and authoritative information in regard to the subject matter within. While every reasonable precaution has been taken in preparation of this book, the author and publisher expressly disclaim responsibility for any errors, omissions, or adverse effects arising from the use or application of the information contained herein. The techniques and suggestions are used at the reader's discretion and are not to be considered a substitute for veterinary care. If you suspect a medical problem consult your veterinarian.

The Leader in Responsible Animal Care for Over 50 Years!™

www.tfhpublications.com

**CENTRAL**
*Garden & Pet*

# Table of Contents

# Chapter 1

# Why I Adore My
# Bichon Frise

Like his very nature, the story of the Bichon Frise, a name that means "curly-coated lap dog," is a happy one. Bright, bold, and bubbly, this snowy sprite of a dog attracts a crowd wherever he goes. Everyone likes this breed, and it's easy to see why. Lovely to look at and delightful to cuddle, the Bichon is one of the easiest and most congenial of dogs to live with.  This clown is all about his people and giving them the giggles every chance he has. He's happiest when folks fuss over him and let him be the life of the party. With an attitude like this, what's not to love?

## History of the Bichon

From royalty to entertainers, people have been drawn to the Bichon Frise and his ancestors for more than 2,000 years. Their small size and fluffy white coats appealed to the aristocracy in the great cities of the world, making the dogs a popular item of barter for goods along the Phoenician trade route linking northern Europe and the Mediterranean lands.

## The Bichon's Beginnings

Although the exact history is a combination of fact and legend, the Bichon family of dogs is supposedly descended from the Barbet, a medium-sized water spaniel–like dog, and other light-colored small dogs. The origin of the Bichon is unknown because so many different colonies of petite milky-coated dogs thrived throughout the world. The Maltese came from Malta; Bolognese from Bologna, Italy; Havanese from Cuba; and the Bichon Tenerife (known as the Bichon Frise today) from the harbor of Tenerife, the largest of the Canary Islands.

All these dogs shared many common traits, but it's their size and coat type that distinguished them from one another. Popular among the nobility for their lap warming and entertaining abilities, the Bichon Tenerife traveled to other areas during the 13th to 15th centuries. The breed was especially desirable in Italy and later in France, particularly throughout the Renaissance. During this time of great cultural change and achievement in Europe, Henry III of France (1551–1589) was so enchanted by his small white furry dogs that it is said he carried a few wherever he went in a tray-like basket hung from his neck by ribbons. Soon after, the ladies of the

*His small size and fluffy white coat have made the Bichon Frise a favored companion for centuries.*

## Bichons in Art

Little white dogs strongly resembling the modern Bichon were depicted in paintings to symbolize the wealth of owners more than 500 years ago. The earliest work featuring a Bichon, the portrait of Federico Gonzaga, Duke of Mantua, by the Italian artist Titian (1500–1540), hangs in the Prado Museum in Madrid.

In the 18th century, portrait artist Sir Joshua Reynolds painted a small, white, curly-coated dog in his *Georgiana, Countess of Spencer and her Daughter*, sometime in 1760 or 1761. A second dog resembling a Bichon appears in another Reynolds painting, *The Ladies Amabel and Mary Jemima Yorke*.

Spanish royal court painter Francisco de Goya frequently included Bichons in his works. His 1793 painting, *Maria Teresa de Borbon y Vallabriga*, today in the National Gallery of Art in Washington D.C., includes a petite, pearly-colored dog sitting on the floor.

During the 19th century, dogs closely resembling Bichons also appear in the artwork of Renoir, Mary Cassatt, and Christine Merrill.

court copied this unique method of toting their favorite dogs with them.

When society reversed positions during the French Revolution (1789-1799), the wealthy and their dogs were tossed out on the street, where only the toughest canines survived. Many accompanied street musicians and tradesmen and had jobs as circus performers. Highly trainable and ever eager to please, agile Bichons were able to walk long distances on their hind legs, wave both paws in the air, and turn somersaults. Today, Bichons spontaneously perform these antics without any training at all.

## The Effects of the World Wars

During World War I, all dogs found it difficult to survive the harsh living conditions, and many breeds perished.

Thanks to a few loyal fanciers who rescued Bichons from the streets of France and Belgium, the breed escaped extinction. In 1933, under the auspices of the Societe Centrale Canine de France (SCCF)—the French Kennel Club—these little dogs were classified by the French as a distinct breed known as the *Bichon a poil Frise* (Bichon Frise), or "Bichon with the curly coat." World War II nearly decimated this hardy breed again, but what remained was a conglomeration of all Bichon varieties.

The Bichon Frise arrived in the United States in 1956, when Mr. and Mrs. François Picault emigrated from France to Milwaukee with their six Bichons in tow and began to breed them. The Picaults met dog fancier Azalea Gascoigne of Milwaukee,

*The Bichon became popular amongst the nobility for his lap warming and entertaining abilities.*

Wisconsin, and Collie breeder Gertrude Fournier of San Diego, California, who became interested in the breed. These were new Bichon breeders who helped to organize other Bichon breeders to form the Bichon Frise Club of America (BFCA).

### The Bichon Frise Club of America (BFCA)

In 1964, the Bichon Frise Club of America (BFCA) was founded. Admitted to the American Kennel Club's (AKC) Miscellaneous Class in 1971, the Bichon was placed in the Non-Sporting Group and became eligible to compete for Championship points in 1973.

### What the Modern-Day Bichon Looks Like

Written by the BFCA, the AKC breed standard of the Bichon Frise describes what the ideal Bichon should look and act like. Every feature of the dog is designed to suggest how cute and bodies that are 25 percent longer than tall. Once heavier-boned than they appear today, the standard prescribes a sturdy medium-boned dog.

There is no such thing as a Toy Bichon. If a breeder is trying to sell you one, be aware of this fact. By definition a Bichon must measure between 9½ and 11½ inches (24.1 and 29.2 cm). No one can look at a puppy and predict what size he will grow up

Bichons are known for the stark contrast of their black eyes, nose, and mouth against their white face.

## Famous Bichon Frise Owners

Famous Bichon Frise owners include Eve Arden, Barbara Taylor Bradford, John Forsythe, Kathy Lee Gifford, Susan Lucci, Sidney and Claire Pollack, Aaron and Candy Spelling, Barbara Streisand, and Betty White.

perky he is. Breeders use this as a blueprint for selecting breeding stock, but what admirers first notice about the breed is the stark contrast of the dog's black eyes, nose, and mouth against his white face.

### Size

The standard stresses balance, with no gross or incapacitating exaggerations, with males and females standing not more than 9½ to 11½ inches (24.1 to 29.2 cm) tall when measured from the ground to the top of the shoulders (withers). Far from delicate, Bichons are robust, with nice round to be. If an adult is smaller than the standard, the dog either has a health problem or is a mixed breed.

## Coat

Coat color ranges from ice white to cream, with the option of apricot or buff shadings around the head, ears, or body. Any shade of white is acceptable as long as it resembles white velvet.

## FAMILY-FRIENDLY TIP

### Bichons and Children: A Good Mix?

Bichons and children can be fast friends. What child doesn't want to cuddle and love a soft, sweet pet? Good family dogs overall, the breed is attracted to the activity and attention that little ones bring, and Bichons are happy to spend time around children. Bichons are gentle, tolerant companions who enjoy sitting on a child's lap and receiving hugs. Small but sturdy, the breed isn't big enough to knock a child over but isn't too fragile, either, although children should be careful with this small dog.

No matter how responsible your child may be, always supervise her around your Bichon. You never know when a lapse in a child's judgment may accidentally injure your dog.

The thick double coat should have a soft, downy undercoat with a coarse, curlier outercoat. It should be very springy and very dense but never flat.

## Head and Neck

The hallmark of the breed is its round head, scissor-trimmed to a perfect circle. The eyes should be round and extremely dark, with a halo of dark pigment around the outer edges. This contrast gives the dog his unique Bichon expression and captures his personality.

Having a long neck that is one-third the length of his body is important because it allows the Bichon to carry his head erect, giving him his perky look.

## Temperament and Behavior

With an independent spirit, the Bichon's cheerful temperament is his most distinguishing behavioral characteristic and the precise quality that makes him a Bichon. Sensitive and affectionate, charming and gentle, with a happy-go-lucky attitude, the Bichon is a lovable dog.

## Companionability

The first sentence of the Bichon breed standard describes the dog's personality perfectly: "The Bichon Frise is a small, sturdy, white powder puff of a dog whose merry temperament is evidenced by his plumed tail carried jauntily over the back and his dark-eyed inquisitive expression."

A companion dog in the truest sense, the Bichon always wants to be the center of attention, and his signature outlook on life is his cheerful attitude. It's this trait that distinguishes the breed from other small white dogs. He's perky but polite, extroverted but well-mannered, and cuddly but quiet.

*The Bichon's cheerful temperament is his most distinguishing behavioral characteristic.*

The Bichon is confident around people, children, and other dogs, and genuinely likes cats, birds, and small household pets such as rabbits, guinea pigs, mice, and birds.

## Environment

This small bundle of fur doesn't need a large home and yard to be happy. With his history as a street performer and a prized pet of the aristocracy, the Bichon will adapt to any city or country household. He's a loyal watchdog who will sound a menacing bark or two or three if someone enters the home who isn't invited, but don't count on him to hold a thief at bay unless it's with kisses. The Bichon will happily greet anyone you allow to enter.

If you can take your Bichon outdoors for exercise, an apartment will suit him just fine. A fenced-in area outside is ideal if you want to let him off the leash, but it's not necessary. He'll enjoy going for a walk, seeing the neighborhood, and meeting new friends.

Leaving your Bichon alone in the backyard by himself for long hours is a bad idea. This breed thrives on companionship, and if abandoned and feeling lonely, your dog may become destructive. Solitary outdoor confinement soon becomes a field of uprooted grass and flower beds, and worse, an invitation to thieves. Bichons are people-pleasers and will happily leave with anyone who comes into the yard.

## Exercise Requirements

Bichons don't require a great deal of exercise. Their short legs are incapable of going the distance, but they do need some activity to keep their minds and

## The Expert Knows

### Is the Bichon Frise Hypoallergenic?

For people who want a dog but are allergic, the Bichon Frise may be one to think about. While every dog has fur, dander, or saliva that may produce allergy symptoms, the Bichon produces less than do other breeds. The best way to find out if you are allergic to a Bichon is to visit a breeder or a friend who has one. Puppy coats are different from adult coats, so try to spend one to two hours holding each one separately.

No matter how much you like the breed's appearance and temperament, consult with your allergist before choosing a Bichon. The last thing you want to do is acquire a Bichon, find out later that you're strongly allergic to your dog, and have to find a new home for him. While a reputable breeder may be willing to take your dog back, it's your responsibility to keep and care for him throughout his lifetime.

bodies stimulated and conditioned. A daily walk and playing ball in the yard is probably enough exercise for your little dynamo. This will keep his bones strong and muscles toned. Don't take your dog walking when it's hot outside because he can easily overheat.

As puppies, Bichons are naturally curious and active, but as they age, they begin to slow down. They will have the occasional burst of energy, spent by zooming around the house—usually in the afternoon, when you're trying to do something quiet yourself.

12

Bichons Frises

*Bichons are playful animals who like to share the fun with other dogs.*

## Playfulness

Ever playful, the breed has a different take than most dogs about what's funny. To Bichons, toys are viewed more as props than as objects to distract them. As long as a family member is nearby to watch his antics, some Bichons have been known to toss a ball into the air, then run to catch it where it bounces, before repeating the trick several more times.

The Bichon is willing to share the fun with other dogs, and once he attracts a playmate, he'll happily begin the game all over again with another toy. It takes an intelligent dog to find things to do, and certainly, the Bichon is as smart as he is lively.

## Trainability

Clever and ever eager to please, the Bichon is a dog who really wants to follow your rules and make you happy. Training a Bichon is no different than training any other dog. It just takes patience, perseverance, and consistency, although having a sense of humor helps, too! For best success, keep lessons short and sweet, and reward your dog's accomplishments with praise or small food treats. Positive reinforcement is the key to lasting learning. Never hit or punish your dog if he makes a mistake. If you do, he'll only resent the bad treatment and act out in other ways.

With his ideal size, winning personality, and glamorous coat, it's no wonder that the Bichon has always enjoyed a favorite spot in the lives of the rich

## SENIOR DOG TIP

### When Is a Bichon Frise a Senior?

Generally, dogs are categorized as seniors when they are seven years old, but because many small dogs live longer than bigger dogs, your Bichon can probably begin his senior citizen status a year or two later. Don't worry—if you feed your dog properly, provide enough exercise and veterinary care, and hug him at least once a day, he'll be with you for a long time.

According to a health survey by the members of the Bichon Frise Club of America, the average lifetime of the Bichon is 14½ years of age, with many living 16 to 18 years. A few have been even older; reportedly, the oldest Bichon died a natural death at about age 21.

and the not-so-rich. Today, he deserves all the care and comfort you can give him, which should be easy. After all, he had you at waving hello.

# Chapter 2

# The Stuff of
# Everyday Life

Your four-footed addition will need a few basics for his new digs, so it's time to go shopping. There's no shortage of dog stuff available, and you'll find everything your Bichon needs through mail-order catalogs, online stores, pet food warehouses, and specialty shops. If you have the time, compare prices because pet supplies are expensive.

**Y**our Bichon will need a variety of supplies, including the following:

- bed
- collar
- crate
- exercise pen
- food, water, bowls
- gate
- grooming supplies
- identification
- leash
- toys

### Bed

Canine snooze spots have come a long way since the early wicker baskets. Today's dog beds are cozy, comfortable, and cute, and you'll see them in all shapes, sizes, and prices. Types range from indoor-outdoor, orthopedic, lounger, molded plastic with a cushion, cot, and designer metal frame. Which one is best for your dog? Your Bichon will have sweet dreams on any of these, so choose something you like.

While you're housetraining him, your Bichon should nap and sleep through the night in a crate. After that, and if he's not a chewer, you may want to give him a puffy dog cushion as a bed for naps during the day.

*Your Bichon's dog bed should be comfortable and safe.*

## Setting Up a Schedule

Taking care of a dog is so much easier if you have a regular routine, with some tasks written on a calendar. This way, you're less likely to forget when it's time to give your dog a bath, trim his nails, brush his teeth, visit the veterinarian, or attend training classes. On a daily basis, feeding, exercising, and grooming your dog at set times reassure him that his life has a certain order to it.

Depending on your home and budget, your Bichon can have one or more beds. For young Bichons who do like to sink their teeth into everything, hold off buying a bed and continue using a crate until he stops chomping.

Choose a small-sized bed cushion that's easy to move around and one with a zip-off replaceable cover that you can pop into the washing machine.

## Collar

Your dog needs a secure-fitting collar for outings on a leash and to hold his identification tags. Because puppies outgrow collars quickly, purchase an inexpensive, lightweight buckle or adjustable quick-release flat, nylon, cloth, or leather one. Don't buy a collar without your puppy, and don't buy one that's too big now, thinking that he will grow into it. Chances are he won't, but in the meantime it can fall off his neck. Carry your puppy into the store and try collars on before buying them to make sure that they fit. With both puppy and adult collars, you should be able to fit two fingers between the collar and your dog's neck.

## Crate

Think of a crate for your Bichon as a crib for a baby. Far from being a jail, it's a safe and cozy place for your dog to rest or hang out in when you can't watch him. A crate is also invaluable when it comes to housetraining because puppies don't like to potty in the area in which they spend time. In addition, it comes in handy if he needs to get away from overactive children or other dogs.

17

The Stuff of Everyday Life

Although it's okay to leave your dog in his crate for a few hours at a time, he shouldn't spend all day, every day, inside while you're at work. A crate is not a place for punishment, either. It's purely for your dog's safety and comfort. Taking your dog in the car for a drive? Put him inside the crate. Like a seat belt for humans, the crate provides protection in case of an accident.

You may have to spend some time training your dog to like his special den (see Chapter 6 for more information), but once he masters this skill, he'll wander inside on his own.

## Types of Crates

There are hard-sided, soft-sided, and wire models from which to choose:

- **Hard sided:** Hard-sided, or molded plastic, crates can be taken apart if necessary and will keep your dog warm in cold weather.

- **Soft sided:** Soft-sided quilted nylon or canvas carriers or carry-on bags are lightweight and easy to take on vacation or to move from room to room.

- **Wire:** The wire crate will keep your dog cool in hot weather. Before you buy one, though, check

*Your Bichon's crate is a secure and cozy place for him to be when you can't watch him.*

it over to make sure that the door and sides fit together securely.

If you're planning to take your dog on an airplane with you, he must stay inside an airline-approved crate or travel carrier.

## Crate Size

The crate should be large enough for your Bichon to stand up and turn around in without hitting his head. A medium-sized crate (approximately 22 inches [55.9 cm] wide by 28 inches [71.1 cm] long by 20 inches [50.8 cm] deep is the ideal side for an average-sized adult Bichon.

If you have a puppy and can only purchase one crate, buy this size. It will be too big for him now, especially when you're trying to housetrain him, but you can block off the back half of it with a crate divider to decrease the size until he's an adult. Puppies do not like to eliminate where they sleep, so if the crate is too big, they'll just go to the far end and do their business there. You also can buy an inexpensive smaller size for your puppy and give it away when he outgrows it.

## Dog Car Seat

For Bichons who like to look out the car window, you may want to purchase a cushioned pet booster seat. There are different types, but look for one that easily attaches to the

## Licensing Your Bichon

When you acquire a Bichon, be aware of dog licensing laws. Some cities restrict the number of dogs living at a residence, and state laws require all dogs to be vaccinated against rabies before they can be licensed. Licensed dogs receive a tag with a city ID number. Attach the tag to your dog's collar. This lets people know that your dog has received a rabies vaccine and where the dog is licensed in case he becomes lost.

By licensing your dog, you are helping to maintain your city's animal shelter and other dog-related services, such as salaries for animal control officers, low-cost neutering clinics, and teaching good pet care to schoolchildren.

seat with a seat belt and that has a shoulder harness. This keeps your dog secure. The dog car seat is an optional item because your dog also can ride in his crate in the car.

### Exercise Pen

A 3-foot-high (0.9-m-high) exercise pen is the perfect enclosure for your Bichon when you have to leave him for several hours. Remove the crate door or prop it

open, and put the crate inside the exercise pen with some toys and a bowl of water. Leave newspaper underneath one corner of it so that your dog can eliminate there. Make sure that the one you buy closes securely and that no sharp edges are present to catch on your dog's coat.

## Food, Water, and Bowls

You'll need two bowls—one that's big enough to hold about 1 cup (236.6 ml) of food and a bigger bowl for water. Both expensive and inexpensive styles are available in plastic, ceramic,

and stainless steel, but if you want to buy bowls that are the easiest to clean and that will last a lifetime, choose stainless steel. Hairline cracks develop in plastic and ceramic bowls, often trapping food bits and collecting bacteria. Bowls with wide bases have less chance of being turned over by your fun-loving Bichon.

## Gate

No matter what your room décor is or what size the entryway is that you'd like to block off, there's a gate to do the job. You'll find gates in hardwood, plastic mesh, and tubular steel, all in a range of colors, widths, and heights. Gates can be configured to enclose large or irregular areas and to serve as barriers for narrow or extra-wide openings. Before shopping, measure the area you're enclosing and determine how high you'd like the gate to be.

## Grooming Supplies

Count on needing a hefty number of grooming tools for your Bichon. (See Chapter 4.) You'll need items for bathing, brushing, clipping, and combing—and don't forget dental and nail care. Buy the highest-quality supplies you can afford because they will do the best job. You're going to have them for a long time, and you want them to last.

## ID Tag/Microchip

Hopefully this will never happen, but in case you and your Bichon ever become separated, an ID tag attached to his collar will help to reunite you. Engraved with your name, address, and telephone number, tags should be easy to read so that anyone who finds your dog can contact you immediately.

Another more permanent form of ID is a microchip, a tiny chip about the size of a grain of rice that is painlessly inserted by a veterinarian

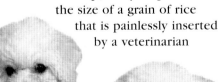

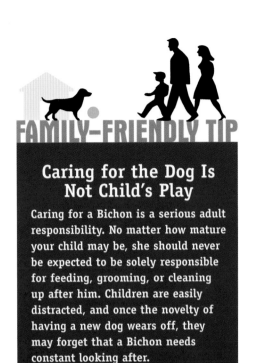

## FAMILY-FRIENDLY TIP

### Caring for the Dog Is Not Child's Play

Caring for a Bichon is a serious adult responsibility. No matter how mature your child may be, she should never be expected to be solely responsible for feeding, grooming, or cleaning up after him. Children are easily distracted, and once the novelty of having a new dog wears off, they may forget that a Bichon needs constant looking after.

Allow your child to assist you with feeding and grooming chores—she will soon become your dog's best friend.

between a dog's shoulder blades. The chip is biologically inactive and contains a series of numbers that can be detected by veterinary and shelter personnel via a handheld scanner. Once the chip is inserted, there's a fee to register it with the manufacturer so that your contact information remains in the manufacturer's ID system.

## Leash

Your Bichon's leash doesn't need to be thick and heavy. A good choice is a thin 4-foot (1.2-m) leather leash. It's sturdy yet lightweight, and will last a

*Your Bichon will enjoy a variety of toys to keep him occupied.*

long time. You'll find web and fabric leashes, which are okay, but they're not as durable. Select a width that's comfortable to hold in your hand.

Whatever you do, don't buy a retractable leash. While this design may look like a good idea, it's very dangerous. Some of these elastic leads extend as far as 12 feet (3.7 m). If your Bichon runs out to the end of this leash and comes face to face with a big, aggressive dog, there's no way you can protect him. This line is also too long to effectively leash train your dog, and if it wraps around someone wearing shorts, it can cut them.

## Toys

Although toys are a real budget buster, buying them is the fun part of choosing dog supplies. Besides amusement, toys keep your dog busy with his own things instead of chewing your furniture or personal items. When puppies are teething, the urge to chew is strong because it relieves pressure on the gums.

You'll find lots of suitable playthings for your Bichon, including toys that talk, squeak, bounce, tug, and challenge his mind. Other toys are chewable, edible, and can be stuffed with treats. Until you know what kind your dog likes, buy the

small size of a few different types. You'll need one or two in each of the rooms in which your Bichon spends time.

Household items make good toys, too, such as empty milk cartons, small plastic water bottles, and cardboard paper towel rolls. Throw them away as soon as your dog begins tearing them up, though. Also, avoid giving your dog your old socks or shoes. Your scent remains in these items, and he'll seek out more of your possessions. To a dog's way of thinking, anything you leave lying around within his reach is fair game for chewing.

Begin giving your dog a few toys as soon as you bring him home, but don't give him everything all at once. Continually rotate them to keep him interested. When you see that he stops playing with one toy, pick it up, put it away, and give him another. If you notice him chewing pieces off, discard that toy so that he doesn't swallow anything harmful.

It's amazing how many things one small dog needs. What you spend on his supplies is probably more than what you paid for him to begin with—but think of his accessories as an investment in his long-term care and education.

## SENIOR DOG TIP

### An Older Dog Comes Home

If you decide to acquire an older Bichon Frise, you may not have to worry about housetraining him or protecting your possessions from his chewing, because he may already be past this stage. He may have just a few bad habits you'll have to retrain, such as nuisance barking or jumping up on guests. That's okay. You're providing a home for a wonderful dog who may have been shuffled around to other homes a few times.

Give your senior a little time to adapt to your routine and to relax and feel comfortable around all family members. Let him take his time acclimating to his surroundings, too. Over the next few days and weeks, introduce him slowly to friends and neighbors. If your dog doesn't want to eat the first meal or two, that's to be expected, but once he realizes that this is his place, you won't be able to remember what life was like pre-Bichon!

# Chapter 3

# Good Eating

Like people, dogs have basic nutritional requirements to keep them healthy. Fortunately, your dog can't go out for fast food or choose the wrong diet for himself. He basically must eat what you give him. His very life depends on the choices you select. Therefore, it's your responsibility to feed him the best food you can afford.

This doesn't mean that you should buy him the most expensive dog food on the market, but it does mean that you must choose the recipe that's the healthiest for him. After all, you want your Bichon to be around for as long as possible, and what he eats is largely responsible for that.

Today, many kinds of dog food are available to please every canine palate. The trick is to select the food that's right for your dog and to make mealtime something to look forward to. Choose a food that's appealing yet contains everything your Bichon needs for good nutrition.

## A Balanced Diet: Nutrients

The dog food you choose for your Bichon should have the phrase "complete and balanced" or "nutritionally complete" somewhere on the label. This translates to having all the nutrients in the prescribed amounts, as required for each growth stage by the American Association of Feed Control Officials (AAFCO). Dog food manufacturers must meet these requirements before receiving AAFCO approval.

Balance is the key to good nutrition, and all nutrients are necessary for good health. Essential nutrients include carbohydrates, fats, minerals, proteins,

*A balanced diet will give your Bichon all the nutrients he needs.*

vitamins, and water. Every nutrient performs a unique function in your dog's body. How he metabolizes it depends on his genetics and environment, how old he is, how much exercise he receives, and if he's under any stress.

## Carbohydrates

Many dry foods contain between 30 and 70 percent carbohydrates. The primary function of most carbohydrates is to provide energy and fiber for proper intestinal function. Carbohydrates include sugars, starches, and dietary fiber, which helps your Bichon with digestion and elimination. Carbs come from cereal grains, such as corn, wheat, rice, and oats.

## Fats

Look for polyunsaturated fats in the dog food you buy. They supply essential fatty acids, which enhance flavor. They also give your Bichon energy, a glossy coat, and a healthy heart. Without enough fats in their diets, many dogs may have skin problems. Too high a fat content and your dog will gain weight. Look for omega-6, omega-3, and linoleic acids as good sources of fatty acids.

## Minerals

Minerals are responsible for healthy bones and teeth, and they help to maintain the body's acid–base, electrolyte, and fluid balances. Trace

## Reading Food Labels

All dog food has two labels on the packages. One is a statement that the food meets or exceeds the nutritional guidelines established by the Association of American Food Control Officials (AAFCO). The other label lists all ingredients in descending order by weight. The major ingredient is listed first, the next highest percentage second, and so on. The AAFCO requirements set the protein levels as 18 percent protein for adult recipes, 22 percent protein for puppy diets, 5 percent fat for adults, and 8 percent fat for puppies. If you have any question about the food, call or e-mail the manufacturer. Its contact information is printed on the label.

elements are minerals that are required in the diet in minute amounts; they serve as essential components of enzymes and hormones. Trace elements include zinc, iron, copper, manganese, cobalt, and iodine. Premium commercial foods fulfill a dog's mineral requirements.

## Proteins

Proteins are made of amino acids, which are the basic elements of cells. The amount of protein in commercial dry foods ranges from about 23 to 26 percent for adult recipes and 26 to 30 percent for puppies. Canned foods have 7 to 9 percent for adult recipes and 9 to 13 percent for puppies. The protein sources in commercial dog

foods are beef, chicken, duck, turkey, venison, eggs, and lamb.

On dog food labels, look for the type of protein. Premium foods use high-quality ingredients that are highly digestible, which account for the higher cost. These do not use meat by-products and usually include at least two different protein sources, listed first and third on the labels. (More than one source signifies a higher percentage of protein, which provides more canine nutrition.) Poorer-quality foods may contain meat by-products, meat- and bonemeal, and animal fat.

## Vitamins

Dogs need a small amount of vitamins in their dog food because they cannot manufacture large quantities to fulfill their daily needs. Fat-soluble vitamins are stored in the body's fat tissues, fat deposits, and liver and consist of vitamins A, D, E, and K. With a potential for buildup, these vitamins can become toxic. Water-soluble vitamins are vitamins B and C, which aren't easily stored by the body and are often lost from foods during cooking or elimination.

Be careful how you store dry dog food. Light, heat, oxidation, moisture, and fat rancidity can destroy vitamins A, E, C, and $B_1$. Keeping dry food in a closed container under normal temperatures maintains freshness.

## Water

Water is important for cellular function and is a vital component of good

# Age-Appropriate Feeding

Feeding your Bichon the right food in the corrrect quantity contributes to good health. Here is a sample feeding schedule to consider (but talk to your veterinarian for recommendations for your particular dog).

| Age | Meals per Day | Recipe Formula |
|-----|---------------|----------------|
| puppies (12 wks to 16 wks) | 3–4 | puppy |
| older puppies (16 wks to 7 mths) | 3 | puppy |
| adolescents (7 mths to 9 mths) | 2–3 | adult |
| adults (9 mths to 7–8 yrs) | 2 | adult |
| seniors (7 to 8 yrs) | 2 | senior |

Unlike larger breeds, Bichon puppies need to eat smaller meals more frequently. They're growing quickly, so feed them a quality puppy food recipe that supplies more protein than an adult recipe. The protein should consist of two different animal proteins, such as chicken, turkey, duck, beef, or lamb, which are listed as the first three ingredients. Depending on their activity levels, adult Bichons will need a total of 2/3 cup (157.7 ml) to 1 cup (236.6 ml) of quality dry food a day.

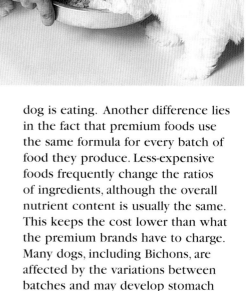

*A diet of dry food is ideal for your Bichon.*

nutrition. Although dogs obtain water from drinking it from their bowls, it's also a component in the food they eat and is obtained from the breakdown of fats, carbohydrates, and proteins. Dogs lose water in hot weather, during extreme exercise, and when experiencing illnesses such as diarrhea, vomiting, and kidney disease. Adding salt to food increases the need for water.

Unless your vet advises otherwise, always make a bowl of fresh cool water available for your Bichon to drink.

## Commercial Food

Walk into any grocery or pet food supply store and you'll find stacks of prepackaged dog food containing different ingredients at different prices. How do you know what to buy? Surely you want to purchase the best food for your Bichon!

Premium-brand dog foods are a better choice for your dog because they often use whole or natural ingredients instead of the fillers or by-products that less expensive foods use. Read the label on the package and you'll know exactly what your dog is eating. Another difference lies in the fact that premium foods use the same formula for every batch of food they produce. Less-expensive foods frequently change the ratios of ingredients, although the overall nutrient content is usually the same. This keeps the cost lower than what the premium brands have to charge. Many dogs, including Bichons, are affected by the variations between batches and may develop stomach upsets and coat problems when given a new batch.

## Dry Food (Kibble)

Small crunchy bites of kibble are the ideal diet for Bichons. Kibble contains 10 percent moisture and all the nutrition your dog needs. Over the last decade, many advances have been made by dog food manufacturers, all in an effort to improve the quality of ingredients. Today, dry dog food is made from a variety of cereal grains or meals, animal or poultry meals, by-products, soybean meal, animal fats, fibers, vitamins, minerals, and preservatives.

One advantage of dry food over canned or semi-moist foods is its convenience. You don't have to refrigerate it, and it can be kept at room temperature. It's easy to pack along for your dog on vacation, and it stays fresh for weeks. Dry food is a good dental cleaner, too, because it helps to scrape down tartar on teeth.

## Semi-Moist Food
Semi-moist food resembles human ground beef patties or meatloaf; while it may look appealing, your Bichon probably won't care what his food looks like as long as it's tasty. Usually found in the freezer section of the pet supply store, semi-moist food is more expensive than dry food, but it's not necessarily better for your Bichon.

Semi-moist food contains 25 to 30 percent moisture and a higher percentage of ingredients that your dog really doesn't need, such as sugar, salt, artificial coloring agents (which may contribute to tearstaining), preservatives, and by-products. The high sugar content contributes to dental disease.

## Canned Food
Canned food is mostly water. The average moisture content is 74 to 78 percent, and the composition varies from meat-based to a high proportion of cereal grain products. This type

of food is the most expensive to feed because it takes more food to supply all the nutrients your dog needs. Many owners mix 1 tablespoon (14.8 ml) of canned food in with their dog's regular dry food to liven up a meal.

Once canned food is opened, it must be refrigerated, so it may not be the best choice to take along on vacations with your dog. It also tends to stick to the teeth and contribute to dental disease.

## Noncommercial Food
Some Bichon owners prefer to make their own dog food rather than buy and serve commercial dry, semi-moist, or dry foods. Home-cooked and raw

## FAMILY-FRIENDLY TIP

### Children and Feeding
Bichons and children are usually close friends, but a child should never be given the sole responsibility of feeding your dog. No matter how mature and capable a child might be, she may not understand what it means to give a dog the right amount of food at every meal, every day. Your child can help by mixing the food in with some water, putting the bowl down, or refilling the water dish with fresh water.

diets have become popular lately, and depending on how much time you have and whether you have the refrigerator and freezer space to store the ingredients, these diets may work for you. The main advantage to raw and home-cooked diets is that you know all the ingredients that your dog is eating and can alter them to suit his likes and dislikes.

### Home-Cooked Diet

Many dog owners derive personal satisfaction from preparing a well-balanced home-cooked diet, and they believe that it is healthier for their dogs than feeding them a commercial dog food. They report that their dogs have more energy and better skin and coat condition.

For a Bichon with a food allergy or sensitivity, or a skin problem, your veterinarian may recommend changing your dog's regular diet to try to pinpoint the trigger food by eliminating one ingredient at a time, then reintroducing it to see if the reaction reappears. Here's where a home-cooked diet that allows you to carefully monitor each ingredient comes in handy.

Your dog needs a complete and balanced meal, not simply your own leftovers. The meal should contain 10 to 30 percent protein (beef, chicken, turkey, lamb, venison, or fish), 25 to 45 percent carbohydrates, including fiber, and the rest should be fats. For Bichons, avoid organ meats, such as the

*A home-cooked diet allows you to more closely monitor what your dog is consuming.*

## Table Manners

Feed your Bichon just one human tidbit from your dinner table and he will never leave the dining room ever again. If you want to stop his begging behavior, don't give him food from your table once you sit down to eat. One alternative is to save healthy leftover pieces of chicken, meat, fruits, or veggies and add them to his food bowl at his next regular meal.

To give your Bichon something to take his mind off your meal, provide him with a rubber toy smeared with peanut butter when you sit down. You also can put him inside his crate or block his entry into the kitchen during mealtime by using a baby gate.

brain, heart, liver, kidneys, and stomach (tripe), as they are too rich and can cause stomach upset. Use olive or sunflower oils for the fat content, and include grains such as rice oats, barley, bran, or wheat. Don't forget fruits and vegetables.

When cooking for your dog, remember to keep your kitchen bacteria-free, and refrigerate and freeze foods properly. Dispose of any leftover food promptly.

To save a little money on food preparation, consider joining other dog owners in a cooperative home-cooked food group. These groups pool their resources and buy raw meat in bulk, rotate responsibilities for food preparation, and share meals with one another. This is a great way to make the process more convenient—and besides, it's fun.

If the prospect of cooking for your dog appeals to you, consult with a veterinary nutritionist to learn what types and amounts of food are good for your Bichon. To find one, ask your

regular veterinarian for a referral, or contact the American College of Veterinary Nutrition (www.acvn.org).

### Raw Diet

The name may not sound appealing, but the BARF diet (Bones and Raw Food or Biologically Appropriate Raw Food) is the ultimate in feeding a noncommercial meal to your dog. It simulates the foods that a dog might eat if he lived in the wild and is based on 60 percent raw, meaty bones and 40 percent pureed vegetables and fresh and dried fruits. Added to that are carbohydrates like barley, oats, rice, or bran.

Dogs love the aroma and taste of the BARF diet, but preparing raw meat has its challenges. It must be served fresh, or if frozen, it should be thawed slowly in the refrigerator and used within two days; never microwave frozen meat to defrost it because that process begins to cook it. Uncooked bones are soft and break down easily during digestion, although bone

Good Eating

*A nutritious diet, in conjunction with exercise, will help to prevent your Bichon from becoming obese.*

34

Bichons Frises

fragments can become lodged in the throat or stomach. If you want to give your Bichon a raw bone, grind it with the meat so that it's easier to consume.

Before you decide to feed your dog a raw diet, talk to your veterinarian. Other health risks are connected with raw meat, such as gastroenteritis, intestinal infection, nausea, diarrhea, and possibly death if the food is contaminated. Raw meat and poultry carry the risk of *E. coli* and *Salmonella*, although, unlike people, dogs are less likely to be affected by these bacteria.

## Supplements

Canine nutritional supplements consisting of vitamins, minerals, enzymes, and amino acids are the latest pet food trend. They claim to improve a dog's health by aiding in digestion, enhancing coat quality, or strengthening bones. While it may sound appealing to increase your dog's well-being, he's already receiving these benefits if he's eating a premium dog food. Today's quality dog food recipes contain these additives in the correct ratios, and adding more can disturb the balance.

Your dog may benefit from fatty acid supplements to improve his skin or from supportive joint compounds to avoid arthritis or joint problems, but consult with your veterinarian before giving them to your dog.

## Treats

There's no shortage of commercial dog food treats to give your dog. Boxes and bags of them fill the shelves of pet food supply stores, and they're advertised everywhere you look. Small bakeries even specialize in making custom treats for dogs. With so many goodies available in all different shapes and flavors, how do you know what to buy?

Look for healthy treats. Read the nutritional analysis, ingredients used, and manufacturer's recommended use listed on the packages. Because treat manufacturers aren't required to meet any standardized nutrient requirements, some treats provide the same nutrition as premium dog food, while others contain more salt, fat, and sugar than your Bichon's regular diet. Avoid commercial treats with chemical preservatives, artificial ingredients, food dyes, and by-products, because they may trigger tearstaining or allergies. Also, avoid giving your Bichon chocolate, onions, and raisins, because these are toxic to dogs.

If you want to prepare your own nibbles, many cookbooks and canine-shaped cookie cutters are available to help you.

Whether you buy or bake your own treats, limit the number you give your dog every day. Extra tasty tidbits shouldn't constitute more than 10 percent of your dog's daily food intake; any more may offset his regular nutrition.

## Free Feeding or Scheduled Feeding?

There are two ways to feed your Bichon: Fill the food bowl with the day's allotment of food and leave it down all day (free feeding), or give your dog his food at scheduled

## SENIOR DOG TIP

### Feeding the Older Dog

As your Bichon ages, his metabolism slows, decreasing his energy and making him more sedentary. His nutritional needs also begin to change. Your veterinarian may recommend switching his diet to a senior recipe containing fewer calories, less fat, and more fiber. Many dog food manufacturers make a senior recipe with moderately restricted levels of high-quality protein, phosphorus, and sodium, and more B vitamins.

You may have noticed that your older dog has either become a picky eater, or he wants to wolf down everything in sight. Many dogs lose their sense of taste and smell and become bored with eating the same food every day. If this is the case with your senior, try mixing in a few interesting and healthy tidbits into his kibble, such as canned food, sodium-free broth, apple, cooked chicken or meat, cottage cheese, or parmesan or low-fat cheddar cheese. Vary these from day to day.

If your dog doesn't finish eating all the food in his bowl, pick it up and discard it after a half hour. Don't give him anything until the next meal. For dogs who are ravenous, you may have to add in a third meal, but make it a small one, and include more cooked vegetables, such as broccoli or green beans.

times, usually twice a day, and pick up the bowl as soon as he's finished (scheduled feeding).

Free feeding may be a good idea if you have a senior dog who takes a long time to eat, but for a healthy dog or a multiple-dog household, it's not a good choice. Food that's left out all day may spoil, attract ants, or lose its flavor. Also, with two or more dogs, there's no way to regulate if one needs a special diet or to know how much food each

one is actually eating. They may even fight over the food. In addition, when food is left out all day for just one dog, you won't know if your dog is too sick to eat or is just being picky.

To encourage good eating habits, pick up the bowl 15 minutes after your dog stops eating and walks away, and don't give him anything else to eat (including treats) until the next meal. After a few days, your Bichon will realize that he needs to either eat it or lose it!

## Obesity

It's not easy to just say no to that sweet little face when he's begging for an extra tidbit in the kitchen, but if your Bichon is already a little chunky, resist the temptation. Here's the best reason why: In all breeds of dogs, obesity is the most prevalent nutrition-related health problem.

Your dog can only eat what you give him, so if you love your dog, keep him at the proper weight and resist overfeeding him. Overweight dogs are prone to developing diabetes, liver dysfunction, cardiovascular and kidney disease, and joint problems, and they have a shorter life span.

Not sure if your Bichon is too fat or too thin? Stand above your dog and look down at his back. Even with his bushy coat, you should be able to see a slightly hourglass-shaped figure and be able to feel his ribs without pressing too hard. There should be a little bit of padding between your fingers and the ribs. You can always consult with your veterinarian about your Bichon's weight and ask her if he needs to lose a few pounds (kg).

If you do put your dog on a diet, gradually cut back on the amount of food you feed him. Add a few cut-up pieces of blanched green beans to his regular food, and take him out for a few more minutes of exercise. An extra walk or some ball chasing may do the trick. Skip the commercial treats, too. Substitute a few berries or bite-sized pieces of melon, apple, or banana for him to chew on.

Whether you decide to give your Bichon premium kibble to eat or make him a home-cooked dinner, feeding your dog the right type and the proper amount of food is one of the best ways to keep him healthy. Don't tolerate begging, even when he entertains you by standing up on his hind legs and waving at you, and never give him scraps from the table. Your reward will be having your Bichon around just a bit longer.

*Every dog loves treats, but be careful not to overdo it!*

# Chapter 4

# Looking Good

When a Bichon Frise is groomed to the nines, he looks spectacular—but this vision of perfection just doesn't happen by itself.  That gorgeous, curly, pearly coat is a tiger to tame and keep under control, and grooming it takes a major commitment of time, energy, and skill.

T his is a high-maintenance breed that requires daily brushing and combing through the coat to prevent matting, a major bath and haircut once a month, and other grooming tasks in between, such as nail trimming, teeth brushing, and ear cleaning. While a professional groomer can help with monthly scissoring, bathing, and brushing, you can perform many of these tasks yourself. Start by assembling all the grooming supplies you'll need ahead of time.

## Grooming Supplies

Purchase quality tools because they will last longer than inexpensive items, and they will make your job much easier.

- anti-static spray solution (tones down flyaway hair)
- baby powder (for working out mats)
- blunt-tipped tweezers (invaluable for tick removal)
- canine toothbrush and toothpaste (a must-have for dental care)
- conditioner (helps to detangle the fur and keeps the skin from becoming too dry)
- cornstarch or styptic pencil (stops bleeding if you cut a nail too far)
- dog grooming scissors (two pairs of high-quality scissors: one blunt-tipped curved and one straight for shaping and trimming)

- electric hair clippers (for shaving off a lot of hair)
- fine-gauge mesh or woman's nylon stocking (to hold back dog's hair when trimming toenails)
- grooming table with grooming noose (raises your dog to your level so that you don't have to bend over during grooming)
- high-velocity pet hair dryer (straightens the hair and gets the job done quickly)

*A grooming table is ideal for keeping your dog steady while you brush and trim him.*

- hydrogen peroxide (cleans wounds and induces vomiting if your dog ingests toxins, foreign objects, drugs, or spoiled food—should always be in your dog's medicine cabinet)
- medicated ear cleaner from your veterinarian
- medium/fine comb with two sets of teeth, one side set close and the other set wider (helps to detangle mats during combing)
- nail clippers
- nonslip bath mat (helps your dog to keep his footing in the tub or sink)
- pin brush with pliable metal bristles set in rubber (use this brush for regular grooming and when drying the coat after bathing)
- shampoo
- slicker brush (for removing debris from the coat and for fluffing)
- towels

## Coat and Skin Care

When should you groom your dog's skin and coat for the first time? Begin training your puppy or adult dog to accept being fussed over the day after you bring him home. Grooming a puppy only takes a few minutes, but it's important to begin setting a routine and training him to like the idea. Have some yummy food treats nearby, and put him up on a grooming table. Remember never to walk away and leave your dog alone on the table. It doesn't take much for him to fall off!

Pet your Bichon and talk to him in a sweet and loving way. Run your hands over his body so that he becomes accustomed to your handling him, and give him a treat. Over the next few grooming sessions, brush him a little longer. Continue to gradually brush him for longer periods until he seems comfortable with the procedure. (You also can clip a few nails at a time to desensitize him to this procedure simultaneously. See section on "Nail Care" to learn how to clip your Bichon's nails.)

## Brushing

The Bichon is one of those unique breeds that seldom sheds. Unlike other breeds that naturally shed their dead hair, the Bichon's dead hair must be removed by combing and brushing. If not, it will mat.

The adult Bichon has a double coat, which consists of a fine, silky-soft undercoat and a puffy, coarse

## Grooming as a Health Check

Grooming time provides the perfect opportunity to find a health issue in its early stages and contact your veterinarian for treatment. Be on the lookout for fleas, ticks, sores, lumps, or other changes. Does your Bichon seem uncomfortable? If so, his skin may feel irritated. Check his ears for odor or infection, and inspect his footpads for cuts, abrasions, or debris.

outercoat. The coarse, or guard, hairs begin to grow along the lower back when your Bichon is about a year old. While the Bichon puppy coat doesn't mat very often, it begins to tangle before his adult coat comes in at about a year of age, especially if it's not brushed and combed out thoroughly every day. Depending on your dog's coat type, it will probably take you 10 to 15 minutes to brush him, or longer if you count the kisses.

### How to Brush Your Bichon

Have your dog lie still on his side on a flat surface, such as a grooming table. This position is ideal. You'll be able to brush those hard-to-reach places (such as under the armpits) more easily, and it's more comfortable for your dog. Give him a toy to play with so that he won't grab at the brush.

Spray the coat with antistatic spray before brushing, which helps to untangle the hair. This prevents the brush from pulling on tangles and minimizes damage to the coat. Use a pin brush to remove most of the small knots or beginning mats. Don't use the slicker brush to remove mats because it will pull out too much of the undercoat and leave the beautiful plush coat looking thin and sparse. Brush the hair up from the skin instead of down against the skin.

On the head, brush the hair toward the face, taking care not to poke your

dog's eye with the pins of the brush. Brush upward along the sides and back, and use the end tooth of the comb to work through any mats or knots. To deal with knots, start at the point farthest from the skin, picking and detangling by working inward.

Comb and then brush the ears, tail, and legs. When you're brushing the ears, brush the underside of the ear first, then the outer side. Because ears and the tail have longer hair, brush the ends first to untangle mats. Next move the brush 1 inch (2.5 cm) or so nearer the body, and remove any tangles there until you are able to freely pull the brush the length of the hair from the skin outward.

## Scissoring
The Bichon's coat grows like a weed and needs to be trimmed or scissored every four to six weeks. Choose between keeping it long in a show clip or shorter in a pet trim. Either way, you'll need to learn how to trim it yourself or hire a good professional groomer to do it.

### Pet or Show Trim?
A pet trim is l/2 inch (1.3 cm) to 2 inches (5.1 cm) long. Other than being a less-sculpted, more casual look, this style attracts less dirt and fewer mats. Because it's the same length all over, you'll spend less time combing, bathing, drying, and brushing this cut.

A show cut is 3 to 4 inches (7.6 to 10.2 cm) long, with

a more sculpted, rounder appearance. Breeders who show their dogs and professional groomers work hard to achieve this style. The legs, head, and neck are shaped differently in certain places. You can learn how to do this, but it takes time and patience. Ask your breeder or a reputable groomer to teach you some of the tricks.

If you decide not to keep your Bichon in a full show coat and prefer the shorter pet trim instead, he can still be scissored to look like a Bichon Frise. By keeping the tail long and flowing, and the ears, beard and mustache short but not shaved or overly scissored, your dog will still retain that unique Bichon appearance.

## Bathing
Active and curious, your Bichon loves nothing better than getting down and dirty in the yard. To keep his coat

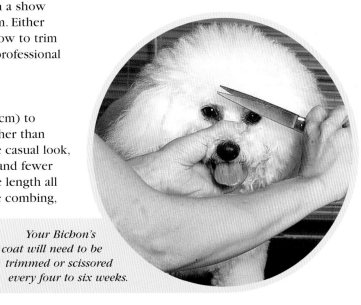

*Your Bichon's coat will need to be trimmed or scissored every four to six weeks.*

sparkling fresh and white, you'll need to clean him off. It's amazing how a little bit of grime can turn a pearly coat gray. If he hasn't had too much fun rolling in a pile of leaves or splashing through the mud, you might be able to get away with just washing his feet and face. At other times, it will take a full-on bath with shampoo and water to restore his ivory glow.

Whether you opt to give your dog the quick rinse-off or the total bath, always brush him free of any knots or mats before getting him wet. Once water mixes with those mats, the knots tighten and the coat is far more difficult to brush out. Assuming your Bichon is more the stay-inside-most-of-the-time kind of guy, you can probably bathe him once every two weeks or even once a

## The Grooming Table

A grooming table with an arm and grooming noose is one of the best accessory investments you'll ever make. It will last a long time and helps with brushing and trimming your dog because it raises him to your height so that you don't have to bend over while grooming him. You also can put a nonskid mat on the kitchen counter, but a grooming table is so much easier!

month. Plan to spend one to two hours for the whole combing, bathing, and brush drying process.

To come clean, your Bichon doesn't need a fancy spa tub because he's compact enough to fit in your kitchen sink, bathtub, or stall shower. Use a nonslip bath mat to prevent him from sliding and injuring himself. To make bathing and rinsing your dog even easier, attach a handheld portable sprayer to the faucet. Use a shampoo formulated for dogs. (Human shampoos have the wrong pH and are harder to rinse out.) It should be thin without lathering up a lot so that it doesn't cause tangling. If you use a coat-brightening shampoo for white dogs, part a

*When bathing your Bichon, aim the sprayer just behind the ears and down the length of his body.*

44

Bichons Frises

section of your dog's hair and look at his skin after bathing. Some Bichons develop skin irritations from these types of shampoos. A lightweight coat conditioner will eliminate static and prevent tangling.

To avoid getting water in your dog's ears, put a small cotton ball inside each ear.

## How to Bathe Your Bichon

Place your Bichon into the tub and use warm water, aiming the sprayer just behind the ears and down the length of his body. Pour a little shampoo along his neck and down his back.

You can use your hand to rub this same shampoo over his chest and between his legs. Massage it in gently, adding some to the top of his head and earflaps. Don't forget the beard and mustache, but keep shampoo out of your dog's eyes. (It will sting and irritate them.)

Rinse the soap out of your dog's coat until the water runs clear. If you're using a conditioner, add it before rinsing completely.

To dry your dog, use a thick towel and squeeze the water out of his coat. Don't rub the hair too much or you will tangle the coat. Towel dry as much as possible. Don't let the coat air-dry because it will droop, curl up, and tangle. Use the pin brush and comb to work out any knots. Then use the slicker brush to brush upward as you blow-dry the coat with a cool setting on the dryer. If the dryer is too hot, it will burn your dog's skin.

## Nail Care

Canine nails grow long quickly. If left unclipped, they continue growing, no matter how much a dog walks on concrete. One poor Bichon brought into a shelter had nails that looked like they had never been cut. They curled under his toes and back into the pads. Don't let this happen to your dog!

*Clip your dog's nails at least every other week.*

## FAMILY-FRIENDLY TIP

### Children and Bichon Grooming

Give your child small jobs to help you groom the dog. This will encourage her participation and teach her how to properly care for a dog. She can gather the supplies, give your dog a treat after nail trimming, and pour on the shampoo and conditioner during bathing. She's also capable of helping you towel dry, put toothpaste on the brush, or talk to the dog while he's being brushed.

Clip your dog's nails at least every other week, preferably before you bathe him. Then you'll be able to wash away any nail fragments that might have been caught between the toes.

To train your dog to relax while you're trimming his nails, begin handling his feet as soon as you bring him home. At least once a day, pick up each foot and gently caress it between both of your hands for a few seconds.

Two types of nail trimmers are available: guillotine and pliers. Everyone has a favorite, so if you don't like the first type, try the other. Some Bichon breeders who show their dogs prefer to use a pet nail grinder instead of nail clippers. The grinder is easier because you can see where the bottom of the quick is before it actually starts to bleed; it's also more precise.

## How to Trim Your Bichon's Nails

For the first few sessions, plan to trim just one or two nails at a time. This beauty treatment can be overwhelming in the beginning, but with time and patience you'll be able to clip all your Bichon's nails.

If you have a table with a grooming noose, or even a picnic table with a nonskid mat, give your Bichon his pedicure up there. It's so much easier than having to hold him and clip at the same time. Choose a time when you know you won't be interrupted, and assemble all the tools you'll need before you put your dog up on the table. Nothing is more aggravating than having to stop clipping because you left the styptic pencil or the net stocking in another room. Have some tasty food treats nearby, too.

First, check between the toes and the pads for any cuts, thorns, or swollen and tender areas. If anything doesn't look right, contact your veterinarian.

Scissor away the excess hair that grows between the pads and on the bottoms of the feet using blunt-tipped scissors. This hair collects debris and mats if it isn't removed. Keeping the pads free of hair helps your dog maintain traction, too.

To trim the nails, lift one paw with one hand and use your thumb and forefinger of the other hand to push back the hair around the nail. If there's too much hair to hold back, try putting a fine-gauge nylon mesh or the toe portion of a nylon stocking over your dog's foot and let the nails poke through it.

Locate the *quick,* or the pink vein that runs the length of the nail. Trim the curved white portion of the nail where the quick ends. If your dog has a few black nails, clip the white nails first so that you know

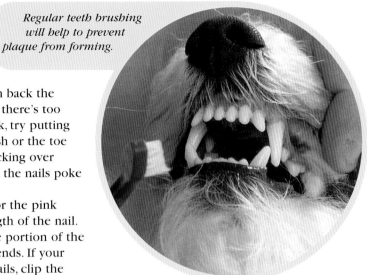

*Regular teeth brushing will help to prevent plaque from forming.*

where the quick might be, then clip the black. Trim off a little at a time. If you go too far, the nail will bleed. In this situation, quickly dab the area with the styptic pencil, or dip your Bichon's foot into a small container of cornstarch. Give him a tasty food treat to soothe his sore foot and his temper at the same time!

Nail trimming takes practice, so don't give up too quickly. It's definitely a skill worth learning because you'll use it forever with any dog you ever have.

## Ear Care

The Bichon's furry ears keep wax and debris trapped inside and prevent air from circulating. These two factors create the ideal location for a raging infection to settle in, making ear care that much more important.

## How to Care for Your Bichon's Ears

To prevent problems, remove some of the long hairs in the ear canal before bathing your Bichon. Use tweezers or your thumb and forefinger to quickly pull out a few excess hairs at a time. It sounds as if this might hurt your Bichon, but the hair isn't deeply embedded, so he will hardly feel it. Once the hair is removed, use a cotton strip or ball

soaked with alcohol or a medicated ear cleaner from your veterinarian to clean out the ear. Don't use a cotton swab because that will just push the debris down deeper. Use the cotton strip or ball to clean the inside of the earflap, and rotate it so that it picks up debris. If there is a lot of dark brown or black wax on the cotton, repeat the process until the cotton comes out clean. Dry out the area thoroughly with an antibacterial powder.

To be on the safe side, pick up your dog's earflaps once a day, check for any offensive odor or a waxy buildup, and clean them if necessary.

## Eye Care and Tearstaining

While some amount of eye tearing is normal, an excessive amount gives many white-coated dogs unattractive brownish stains beneath their eyes. There are many reasons for this discoloration: dog food additives, mineral deposits in tap or soft drinking water, or airborne allergies. Ingrown eyelashes, yeast infections, or bacteria in the tear ducts also can be the culprits.

Many products in the aisles of pet supply stores claim to prevent, stop, or cover tearstains up, but these products don't treat the source of the problem. To determine the exact cause, ask your veterinarian to examine your dog's eyes and eyelashes.

## How to Care for Your Bichon's Eyes

Once your veterinarian gives your dog's under-eye stains a normal bill of

**SENIOR DOG TIP**

### Grooming the Senior Bichon

As your Bichon ages, it's just as important to maintain his regular grooming schedule, especially brushing his teeth every day and having them professionally cleaned by your veterinarian every few months.

If your dog isn't as tolerant as he once was during brushing or nail trimming, give him a few tasty treats to motivate him. He may have sensitive skin, too, so take a little more time and be extra gentle with him. For example, don't brush his coat too hard. (His coat may be thinner, so there may be fewer mats anyway.)

health, keep the corners and the areas beneath the eyes clean every day. Trim the hair away from the area around the eyes every week or more often if it grows in quickly. Use a cotton ball and warm water to wash the area every day. Or instead of using water to wash the eye area, some Bichon breeders use a mixture of one part hydrogen peroxide to two parts water and carefully apply it with a cotton swab underneath the eye before drying the area thoroughly with a cotton ball. Finally, they dab a little petroleum jelly

beneath the eye, which protects the delicate coat from staining.

## Dental Care

Like people, your Bichon's teeth need to be kept clean. Veterinarians recommend brushing your dog's teeth once or twice a day, or at least a few times weekly. Brushing prevents plaque (which turns into calculus) from forming and extending under the gum line, forming pockets that allow bacteria to thrive.

Rather than a human toothbrush and toothpaste, use a canine toothbrush or a rubber canine finger brush. These are specially designed to fit a dog's mouth. Canine toothpaste contains enzymes to dissolve plaque before it hardens into calculus, and it doesn't need to be rinsed. Besides, your Bichon will love the taste!

### How to Clean Your Bichon's Teeth

Begin training your Bichon to accept brushing the day after you bring him home. Put a little of the toothpaste on your finger and rub it over one or two of his teeth. He will try to lick it off, but that's okay. After a few sessions, you'll be able to put the paste directly on the brush, and he'll allow you to clean all his teeth.

For a more thorough cleaning, have your dog's teeth professionally cleaned by the veterinarian once or twice a year. Another way to avoid dental disease is to feed your pet a good-quality dry dog food, which helps to scrape down calculus. Avoid feeding only wet food because it sticks to the teeth.

## Finding a Professional Groomer

When searching for a professional groomer, ask your veterinarian, breeder, or dog-owning friends for referrals. Before making any grooming appointments, though, visit shops to meet the owners and tour the facilities. Shops should be clean and odor-free, and the staff neat and professionally dressed. Potential groomers should know that the Bichon has specific styling and coat needs.

Here's a list of questions to ask groomers:

1. **What kind of dryer do you use?** Bichons needs to be blown dry by hand rather than with a cage dryer, which may cause your dog to overheat.

2. **What certification do you have, and do you have references?**

The groomer should be certified and experienced. Groomers' associations, such as the National Dog Groomers Association of America, Inc. (NDGAA) and the International Society of Canine Cosmetologists (ISCC), award Master Groomer certification after an education and testing process.

*Your Bichon's professional groomer should understand his coat and styling needs.*

3. **What experience do you have with Bichons?** Does the owner or any of the staff go to dog shows? Your groomer should know the Bichon breed standard and how the breed should look.

4. **What weekly and monthly maintenance schedules do you recommend?** Depending on how much work you want to do between visits, your Bichon will need a regular schedule to keep up with coat demands.

5. **What is your least busy day?** Schedule your appointment for that day so that your groomer will have enough time for skillful scissoring without being rushed.

Once you choose a groomer, show her a photo of what you want your dog to look like. If you like this professional, request the same one every time.

Once you learn how to manage the whole grooming routine, you and your dog will begin to look forward to spending quality time together. Regularly sprucing up your dog is a responsibility, but the reward for all your hard work is having a healthy dog. Besides, you'll receive lots of extra Bichon kisses.

# Chapter 5

# Feeling Good

It's hard to imagine a robust Bichon feeling under the weather, but sometimes it happens. As with every breed of dog, Bichons are not immune to general illnesses and genetic diseases. But with good veterinary care and close observation, you often can detect problems early enough to obtain treatment. Keep in mind that Bichons are basically a very healthy breed, and when well bred and well cared for, can live a long time.

*Bichons are generally a healthy breed and have the potential to live a long time.*

## Veterinary Care

One of the best things you can do for your Bichon is to provide him with regular, quality veterinary treatment.

### Finding a Veterinarian

Look for a compassionate, knowledgeable veterinarian who explains everything clearly. To find one, ask your breeder, other dog owners, your local shelter, or canine professionals such as groomers, trainers, or the American Animal Hospital Association (AAHA) for recommendations.

Veterinarians don't specialize in particular breeds, although they should be familiar with the common health issues that Bichons suffer from. Schedule a visit to the clinic before your dog has a problem, meet with the veterinarian, and see if the clinic is clean. If you're comfortable with the professional you've chosen, your dog will be, too.

### Regular Veterinary Visits

How often does your Bichon need to see the veterinarian? Schedule the first visit within 24 to 72 hours of bringing him home, with follow-up appointments once or twice a year. During routine exams, the veterinarian will monitor your Bichon's

# SENIOR DOG TIP

## How to Support Your Senior's Health

The Bichon Frise is a playful, hardy breed, so you may not even notice him slowing down that much. Then, one day, he may lose a little urinary or bowel control, show little interest in his meals or crave food, and even be less active.

Continue brushing your Bichon's teeth every day and have his teeth professionally cleaned, although you may have to schedule a few extra visits to keep the tartar and plaque levels down. Check his ears to make sure that they are free of infection, and keep your dog's toenails as short as possible. He's not so steady on his feet, and if his nails are too long, his ability to walk will be hampered.

Climbing stairs might be difficult for him, so pick him up and carry him. To keep him limber, walk him regularly, give him an extra cushion in his bed, and make sure that he's warm enough during cold weather.

Take your dog to the veterinarian twice a year. Many veterinarians offer special senior checkups that include a complete blood panel, listening to your dog's heart, and taking his temperature. These are your Bichon's golden years, and the best thing you can do for him is to continue visiting the veterinarian regularly. Tell her about any new conditions your dog develops. She can suggest treatments or medications to keep him comfortable in his old age.

*Ask your veterinarian what vaccines are right for your Bichon.*

temperature and weight, examine his heart and lungs, and check his eyes, ears, mouth and teeth, skin, and coat. Your Bichon's teeth also should be cleaned twice a year.

Routine exams are important because they give your vet the opportunity to spot problems in their early stages and to perform laboratory tests before making a diagnosis. If you have any questions about your dog's health or behavior, feel free to ask the doctor.

## Vaccinations

Traditionally, dogs have been vaccinated once a year to protect them against fatal and life-threatening infectious diseases, but that schedule has been revised. Research veterinarians and Bichon breeders believe that a connection exists between autoimmune diseases causing

disabling, chronic illness, and overvaccination for all dogs as well as Bichons.

## Vaccination Guidelines

To establish standard guidelines, the American Animal Hospital Association (AAHA) issued a set of vaccination guidelines recommending four essential vaccines for every dog: canine distemper virus, canine parvovirus, canine adenovirus-2, and rabies. Other than rabies, which local laws dictate when it must be given, the AAHA recommends vaccinating puppies at 6 to 8 weeks, 9 to 11 weeks, and 12 to 14 weeks, with an initial "adult" vaccination given when the dog is older than 16 weeks. Two doses, three to four weeks apart, are advised, but one dose is considered protective and acceptable. The guidelines also recommend giving a booster shot when the dog is one year old and giving a subsequent booster shot every three years, unless risk factors are present that make it necessary to vaccinate more or less often.

Vaccines against the distemper-measles virus, canine parainfluenza virus, leptospirosis, *Bordetella bronchiseptica*, and *Borrelia burgdorferi* (Lyme disease) should only be given to dogs who risk exposure because of the geographic area in which they live, their lifestyle, or their travel habits. For giardia, canine coronavirus, and canine adenovirus-1, vaccines are not generally recommended because these diseases pose little risk to dogs, are easily treatable, or the vaccine has not been proved effective.

## When to Vaccinate

A titer test (via a blood draw) measures the level of antibodies already present in the blood to protect a dog against disease. Many veterinarians and Bichon breeders run titers so that they know for sure if and when their dog needs a vaccine.

## When to Revaccinate

If your dog needs both his rabies vaccine and the combination vaccine (DA2PP), another vaccine, the Bichon Frise Club of America (BFCA) strongly recommends not giving both at the same time because this can stress a dog's immune system. To decide what vaccines your Bichon needs and how often they should be given, talk to your veterinarian about running a titer test

(via a blood draw), which measures the level of antibodies already present in the blood that protect a dog against disease. Many veterinarians and Bichon breeders run titers so that they know for sure if their dog needs a vaccine. Together you can safeguard your dog's health.

## Neutering (Spaying and Castrating)

If you bought your Bichon from a responsible breeder, you will be asked

## FAMILY-FRIENDLY TIP

### How to Prepare Your Child for a Vet Visit

To help your child prepare for a vet visit, explain what the experience might be like, and tell her that she must stay away from other dogs in the office because they may bite. Explain that you expect your child to sit quietly with you and wait, rather than running around the office making a lot of noise.

If your child has a small toy, bring it to keep her busy because the visit might take a while. Maybe she can help you hold your dog's leash, but explain that you must be in charge at the office. Your Bichon may be excited or shy, and he will need an adult to reassure him.

> *Neutering your Bichon is a responsible act that helps to alleviate the problem of unwanted dogs.*

to sign a spay-neuter agreement. This is the breeder's way to safeguard future generations of the breed. The last thing you want to do as a responsible Bichon owner is to contribute to the pet overpopulation problem. By signing the agreement, you are leaving breeding to the serious, ethical breeders who have spent their lives studying the breed.

The best way to prevent puppies is to have your female spayed (removal of the ovaries and uterus) or your male castrated (removal of the testicles). These surgical procedures also help to reduce the chance of your dog developing cancers of the reproductive system.

Spay your female before her first season, usually by eight months of age, and you'll reduce the risk of breast cancer. If she doesn't go into heat, you won't have to worry about a mess in the house. Your male should be neutered before he is one year old to avoid prostate problems later on. The procedure also will deter him from marking in the house or from looking for females in season in the neighborhood.

## Parasites

Keeping your Bichon parasite-free is an important part of maintaining his good health. If left untreated, the two types of parasites—external and internal—reproduce rapidly and cause infestation. Parasites are irritating, making your dog's life miserable and weakening his health.

### External Parasites

Fleas, mites, and ticks are external parasites that live on or near the skin.

#### Fleas

Aside from being common and annoying, fleas and their saliva can cause highly allergic reactions in Bichons that can make your dog's life miserable.

Just because fleas multiply like crazy in grassy areas, carpeting, and bedding doesn't mean that your dog has to host them. Today there are many ways to keep your dog pest-free, although many Bichons can be allergic to flea-killing products. Discuss with your veterinarian what products are safe to use on your dog.

#### Mites

Different types of these microscopic arachnids are responsible for sarcoptic mange, demodectic mange, ear mites, and cheyletiella.

- **Sarcoptic mange** is caused by the scabies mite. The female scabies mite burrows into the skin and lays eggs, which hatch into larvae, causing lesions and secondary infections on an affected dog. Symptoms of sarcoptic mange include matted hair and crusty skin. Take your dog to the vet, who will examine the area and prescribe a medicated shampoo and an insecticide.

- **Demodectic mange** mites are always present on your dog, but his immune system prevents them from doing any harm. However, if the immune system is weak, the mites can move into hair follicles and cause a dog's hair to fall out. A medicated dip can clear up this condition, but it may take several months.

- **Ear mites** work their way into the external ear and the ear canal. If your dog shakes his head and tries to rub his head and ears on the ground, he may have ear mites. Symptoms of ear mites include a dark discharge and odor from the ear. Your veterinarian can diagnose the problem and thoroughly clean the ear with medicated ear drops.

- **Cheyletiella**, also known as walking dandruff, produces hair loss, but it's not irritating to your dog. Your veterinarian can prescribe a special pesticide to clear up the condition.

To diagnose the type of mite, your veterinarian can examine a skin scraping of the affected area and prescribe a medicated dip to kill the mites.

### Ticks

Ticks transmit Lyme disease, Rocky Mountain spotted fever, and ehrlichiosis. They live in bushy, mountainous areas and attach themselves to a dog's chest, ears, inner thighs, and neck, surviving on their blood.

Because Bichons spend much of their time in the house, their chance of coming in contact with ticks is slim. To be on the safe side, though, always check for ticks after your dog returns from an outing and when you groom him.

If you find a tick on your dog, don't panic. Calmly get your first-aid kit and assemble your supplies: jar of alcohol, tweezers, and latex gloves. Separate the hair around the tick, or use the flea comb to find where the tick is attached. Using the tweezers, carefully lift the tick's head and pluck it out quickly without crushing it. Dunk it into the alcohol to kill it or flush it down the toilet. Clean the area with some hydrogen peroxide and antibiotic ointment, and wash your hands. If a welt remains where the tick was, it will subside. If not, take your dog to your veterinarian because it may be infected.

Tick preventives are available, but ask your veterinarian whether you should use them, because many Bichons are allergic to these chemicals. If you do use a preventive, watch your dog closely for any adverse skin reactions that might occur, such as itching or hives, and notify your veterinarian immediately.

*Check your dog for fleas and ticks after he's been playing outside.*

## Internal Parasites

Despite the best attempts to prevent them with deworming medications, intestinal parasites are sometimes passed from a mother to her puppies during pregnancy. In newborn pups and in some adult dogs, they can cause anemia, diarrhea, weight loss, and vomiting. To identify the parasite, take a stool sample to your veterinarian.

## Heartworms

The bite of an infected mosquito is all it takes to transmit heartworms. The worms' larvae travel through the bloodstream to the dog's heart and are deadly within a few months. Signs of infestation include coughing, weakness, lethargy, and shortness of breath. Your Bichon's blood should be tested for the presence of heartworm microfilarie. If none are present, give him a monthly preventive, which is also effective for other types of worms.

## Hookworms

Small hookworms attach themselves to a dog's intestinal wall and can cause anemia, bloody diarrhea, weight loss, and weakness. They are carried from the feces of infected animals.

## Ringworm

Ringworm is a fungal infection that has nothing to do with a worm. It infects the skin and hair and appears as a red,

### Should You Insure Your Dog?

For people, having health insurance can save a great deal of money in medical bills. For dogs, that may not be the case. With veterinary insurance, policyholders pay their veterinarian directly and file a claim for reimbursement with their insurance company.
Before signing up for pet insurance, read the policy carefully to find out what procedures will or won't be covered and if the policy includes Bichon health problems. Premiums usually cost more for older dogs, and not all costs are reimbursed, so pet health insurance may not be worthwhile in the long run.

rough, and crusty circle of skin with broken hairs and hair loss. Puppies are more susceptible to this infection, which is usually spread by coming into contact with an infected animal. Antifungal medication is effective in treating ringworm, although it eventually disappears on its own.

## Roundworms

Most puppies are born with roundworms. Present in the stool, they look like long strands of spaghetti. They cause watery diarrhea, a dull coat, failure to thrive, and even death unless puppies receive deworming medication.

Feeling Good

*Food allergies can be caused by a variety of ingredients, including artificial coloring, fillers, and preservatives.*

### Whipworms

These 3-inch (7.6-cm) worms resemble a whip and can live in a dog's large intestine. They're responsible for foul-smelling diarrhea and are hard to kill. Pick up your dog's feces every day to avoid reinfestation, because whipworms can survive in infected soil for years.

### Breed-Specific Illnesses in Bichons

All dogs have genetic health issues, and Bichons are no exception. According to the BFCA, some of the most common health problems in the Bichon include:

1) allergies
2) bladder stones
3) cancers
4) cataracts
5) Cushing's disease
6) dental problems
7) hip dysplasia
8) Legg-Calve-Perthes Disease
9) patellar luxation

Ethical breeders are aware of these issues and perform genetic tests on dogs whom they breed to screen out problems in future generations.

### Allergies

According to the BFCA, skin allergy is the most common health disease in Bichons. Nearly half of all Bichons need sporadic allergy treatments sometime during their lives, and a small percentage has serious allergy problems. The environment and heredity are responsible. Several types of allergies are possible: inhalant allergy, flea allergy, and food allergy.

### Symptoms

Exposure to an allergic substance causes an immune response, and the dog's skin releases compounds that cause it to itch. With inhalant and food allergies (which can be caused by beef, chicken, dairy, soy, corn, wheat, artificial coloring, fillers, or preservatives), the itch results in chewing and licking paws, scratching around the face, hair loss, and red skin.

Flea allergies produce itching around the base of the tail and also over the entire body.

### Treatment

A veterinary allergy specialist can perform skin testing to determine what your Bichon is allergic to. Once she knows the cause of the allergy, she can prescribe treatment.

## Bladder Stones

When stones are present in the urinary tract, they can cause a blockage in the urethra. Bichons can develop two types of stones: calcium oxalate, which are genetic; and struvite, which are not genetic and are caused by diet and/or bladder infection, lack of water, or inability to urinate. Bichons must have frequent opportunities to empty their bladders; they also should receive regular exercise and be given constant access to drinking water.

### Symptoms

Symptoms of bladder stones include straining to urinate, distention of the bladder, urinating small amounts of urine or dribbling, nausea, whimpering, or cloudy or bloody urine.

### Treatment

Calcium oxalate stones only can be removed with surgery. Struvite stones can be dissolved using a diet low in certain types of protein, antibiotics, and vitamin C.

## Cancers

The word "cancer" strikes fear in every dog owner's mind, but many advances have been made in the treatment of this deadly disease. Recognizing it early, obtaining an accurate diagnosis, and carefully planned therapy can help to manage cancer.

### Symptoms

There are 12 warning signs:

1) abnormal swellings that continue to grow, especially in the lymph nodes

2) sores that do not heal

3) bleeding or discharge from the mouth, nose, urinary tract, vagina, or rectum

4) offensive odor

5) difficulty eating and/or swallowing

6) difficulty breathing

7) difficulty urinating or defeating

8) hesitation to exercise, or loss of energy

9) loss of appetite, weight loss

63

You never know when your dog will have an emergency. Having a first-aid kit available to help him can often mean the difference between saving your dog's life and losing him. This kit doesn't need to be fancy. All you need is a plastic container that's large enough to hold everything you may need in case of emergency:

- ASPCA Animal Poison Control Center's phone number: 888 426-4435

- after-hours emergency clinic phone number

- antibiotic ointment—use on a wound after cleaning

- antidiarrheal medication—for first 24 hours only; after that, contact your veterinarian

- antiseptic and antibacterial baby cleansing wipes—great for cleaning up wounds while away from home

- antihistamine—for bee stings and spider bites; notify your veterinarian and ask correct dosage

- digital rectal thermometer—if you have an old mercury thermometer, discard it because it may leak dangerous fluid; when you take your dog's temperature, write it down so that you can remember it later

- ear cleaner—for wiping out ears

- flea comb—fine tooth for flea and tick removal

- gloves—thin latex is best to avoid contamination or to remove ticks

- hydrogen peroxide 3% solution—for cleaning wounds and wiping away blood

- instant cold compress—for cooling your dog down if he overheats

- jar of alcohol—for tick collection

- muzzle or gauze roll—to protect you if your dog is in pain and bites you accidentally.

- nonstick adhesive tape or vet wrap— keeps gauze bandages in place easily

- paper and pen—a small spiral notebook for making notes about the injury; your veterinarian might ask you questions later on

- rubbing alcohol—clean the thermometer before using it

- saline eye solution—for flushing out any eye irritants

- small scissors—to cut bandages

- sterile cotton balls or rolled cotton, sterile gauze pads—to stop bleeding and for cleaning the wound

- towels and washcloths—for washing affected areas

- tweezers—for removing ticks

- veterinary first-aid manual

- your veterinarian's phone number

10) persistent lameness or stiffness of movement

11) lumps in the breast area

12) abnormality or difference in size of testicles

## Treatment

Traditional forms of treatment include surgery, radiation therapy, and chemotherapy. New and alternative technologies requiring specialized equipment include freezing tumor tissue, heating tumors, lasers, and immune system enhancers.

## Cataracts

A cataract is a cloudiness of the eye lens or the membrane that surrounds it. Cataracts are inherited and can cause blindness in fewer than 10 percent of all Bichons as young as one year or sometime before their seventh birthday. Another 30 to 40 percent of all Bichons may be carriers. The BFCA recommends that breeders should know that at least several generations of ancestors have been tested clear of cataracts and registered with the Certified Eye Registration Foundation (CERF) before breeding adult dogs.

## Symptoms

Cataracts are often detected when the eye looks cloudy.

## Treatment

Today, some of the same cataract treatments available for people are also being used on dogs. Surgical removal of the lens offers the best treatment, with recent advances in surgical techniques and equipment yielding excellent results.

## Cushing's Disease

Middle-aged Bichons most often develop Cushing's disease, or hyperadrenocorticism, which is the overproduction of the hormone cortisol. (This hormone helps the body respond to stress.) Using too much cortisone to manage allergy symptoms may be responsible.

## Symptoms

Symptoms of Cushing's disease include weakness, low body temperature, loss of appetite, hair loss, vomiting and weight loss, and increased thirst and urination.

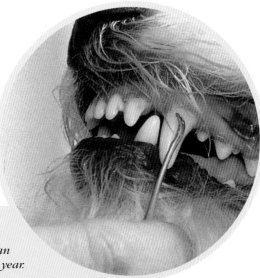

*Bichons require dental scaling by a veterinary technician a few times a year.*

### Treatment

Constant monitoring and medication is needed to maintain healthy cortisol hormone balances.

### Dental

Most toy dogs have tiny mouths with little room for teeth. Crowded together, a Bichon's teeth can cause dental problems such as deformity, gingivitis, premature decay, and retained baby teeth that must be extracted. Often, you'll see food stuck between the teeth.

### Symptoms

If you notice bad breath, red or swollen gums, or bleeding, your Bichon needs to visit the veterinarian. Tartar and plaque builds up and causes gingivitis, or inflammation of the gums, leading to bone deterioration and tooth loss.

### Treatment

Bichons need their teeth brushed every day, and they require dental scaling by a veterinary technician a few times a year. To treat periodontal disease, veterinarians can prescribe antibiotics and perform a variety of techniques, including scaling, root planing, subgingival curettage, polishing, and extraction.

### Hip Dysplasia

Hip dysplasia is caused by an abnormal formation of the hip, leading to looseness in the hip joint. The looseness creates abnormal wear and erosion of the joint, and as a result, pain and arthritis develop. Carrying around extra weight exacerbates the degeneration of the joint. Many breeds suffer from this crippling orthopedic disease.

### Symptoms

Some dogs who are dysplastic may not show any signs until middle or old age, although a young dog who is severely affected with dysplasia may have trouble climbing stairs, jumping up, or

*If your Bichon seems unusually lethargic, contact your veterinarian.*

running around the house. Other signs of dysplasia include running with both back legs nearly together, resembling a rabbit, and difficulty arising.

### Treatment
Pelvic X-rays reveal the presence or absence of the malformation; surgery can correct the problem.

## Legg-Calve-Perthes Disease
This crippling hereditary disease in young toy dogs is occasionally diagnosed in Bichons as young as four to six months of age. It is caused by a reduction of the blood supply to the maturing femoral head in the hip joint. Because of the lack of blood supply, the bone dies, leaving the hip joint misshapen.

### Symptoms
This is a very painful disease that causes limping at the onset and inability to use the leg in later stages.

### Treatment
Surgical removal of the diseased bone is possible and usually successful.

## Patellar Luxation (Slipped Kneecap)
A slipped kneecap is the leading orthopedic hereditary problem in Bichons. When the femur (long thighbone) develops abnormally, it strains the thigh muscle attached to the patella (kneecap). The knee joint's bones and ligaments soon become deformed. At the same time, the groove in the thigh bone may not be deep enough to hold the kneecap in place, causing it to slip out of the joint. Degrees of patellar luxation are labeled Grades 1, 2, 3, or 4, with 4 being the most severe.

Bichons should never be allowed to jump off high places, such as a bed or couch, onto the floor, because this stresses the kneecap.

### Symptoms
If your dog skips instead of walking or running, he may have a slipped kneecap.

### Treatment
Surgery may be needed to repair and realign the joint.

## General Illnesses
Dogs get sick from time to time. It's a fact. As soon as you notice trouble brewing, it's time for action to restore your dog's health.

## Diarrhea
Get in the habit of observing your dog's bowel movements at least once a day. Stools should not be loose or runny, bloody, or mucus-like. There are many reasons for these unusual stools, but if they last longer than a day, contact your veterinarian and ask whether you should change your dog's diet or if medication is needed.

## Ear Infections
Beneath that snowy head of downy soft hair are your dog's ears. At least once a week, pick up the earflap

## What Is a Holistic Veterinarian?

A traditional veterinarian considers a dog's physical symptoms before making a diagnosis and recommending treatment. A holistic veterinarian evaluates the total dog by considering his body, environment, genetics, mind, and spirit. She will study his recent medical and dietary history and will want to know if he has suffered emotional stress or has exhibited any abnormal behavior. Treatment is based on a wide range of therapies that may include minimally invasive techniques as well as acupuncture or homeopathy.

To find a holistic veterinarian in your area, contact the American Holistic Veterinary Medical Association (AHVMA) at www.ahvma.org.

and check underneath for redness, swelling, or a dark discharge in the inner ear folds. This could mean an ear infection, possibly caused by an allergy. Ask your veterinarian to examine the ear and to show you how to clean your dog's ears. A clean ear is usually a healthy ear.

### Eye Infections

Bichons are fairly low to the ground, which means that their eyes can come in contact with foreign objects, such as thorny rose bushes. One scratch can irritate the eye, causing infection, and eventually damaging the cornea. Keep your dog away from sharp plants and other objects, and observe if his eyes are red, swollen, or have a discharge. An allergy or a clogged tear duct could be responsible. Contact your veterinarian, who may refer you to a veterinary ophthalmologist for diagnosis and treatment.

### Vomiting

At least once in your dog's lifetime, he's going to have an upset stomach and vomit. Hopefully, it won't be on your down comforter or antique rug. One mess isn't usually a problem, but several incidences of vomiting are cause for concern. Keep a log of the date and time of the vomiting, and contact your veterinarian.

### Alternative Therapies

Today's veterinary medicine incorporates a variety of traditional and modern methods to improve canine health. The emphasis is on treating the whole dog rather than just treating one aspect of illness. Choosing techniques that minimize the dog's stress and discomfort during treatment is a priority.

### Acupuncture

Acupuncture is one part of a body of ancient Chinese methods of diagnosis and treatment called *traditional Chinese medicine*. The veterinary acupuncturist applies small-gauge needles to various points on the dog's body to rebalance energy. The technique alleviates pain and attempts to heal nervous disorders, skin disease, skeletal abnormalities, and reproductive problems. Early records show that Stone Age humans used fish-bone needles in China 5,000 years ago.

To find a veterinarian who practices acupuncture in your area, contact the American Academy of Veterinary Acupuncture (AAVA) at www.aava.org.

## Chiropractic Care

If your dog somehow injures himself, his skeletal structure can become misaligned, resulting in pain. A veterinary chiropractor manipulates the spine to restore correct alignment.

To locate a veterinary chiropractor, contact the American Veterinary Chiropractic Association (AVCA) at www.animalchiropractic.org.

## Homeopathy

In homeopathy, diluted amounts of natural materials (animal, mineral, and herbal) are used to stimulate the body's immune system against very specific immune-body responses, such as seizures, cancer, lumps and bumps, and allergic responses (asthma, bronchitis, sneezing, discharges). This works similarly to a vaccine or anti-allergy serum injection.

To find a homeopathic veterinarian, contact the Academy of Veterinary Homeopathy (AVH) at www.theavh.org.

## Massage Therapy

A good massage works wonders if your Bichon is feeling stressed and achy. Hands-on, deep-tissue techniques increase circulation, reduce muscle spasms, and promote healing. Petting your dog goes a long way, and you can learn some of these massage methods yourself through books on the subject.

Many new treatments and techniques are available to keep your Bichon healthy. Adopt the habit of observing your dog every day. Notice his behavior, and if he does anything differently, such as limping, skipping meals, or suffering in silence, that's your tip-off that your dog may not be feeling well and may need to visit the veterinarian. With the right health care, though, your Bichon will be with you for many years.

Feeling Good

*Observe your dog every day for changes in behavior that may signify illness.*

# Chapter 6

# Being Good

While it's natural to want to pick up your dog every time he gets into trouble, training him is a lot easier in the long run.  Teach your Bichon the limits of the household, and you'll always have a dog who's a pleasure to live with.  Training doesn't ruin his spirit; it builds his confidence because he knows what to expect.

## Why Train Your Bichon?

The Bichon Frise is a popular breed, and you'll see Bichons wherever you go. Their small size and lively personality make it easy to take them on outings. While some Bichons are model canines, others need some training. Sure, the breed is pleasing to look at, but no one appreciates a Bichon behaving badly, no matter how pretty your dog may be.

Just as no one likes a spoiled child, no one appreciates a bratty dog. Large or small, all dogs must understand that there are household and social rules they must live by. Once your Bichon knows the limits, he'll be happier because he knows exactly what his place in the world is.

Out in public, your dog is an ambassador of goodwill for his breed and for all dogs. It helps if he knows how to behave around people and other dogs and is welcomed nearly everywhere.

## Socialization

Bichons are the social butterflies of the dog world. Their genetic makeup dictates that the more human contact they have, the better off they are. To help your dog fulfill what he was born to do, socialize him as soon as you bring him home. By exposing him to a variety of people, animals, sights, sounds, and objects, he'll have the opportunity to trust the environment and realize that the world is a very happy place. Dogs who never leave the house are likely to grow up fearful or aggressive.

## How to Socialize Your Bichon

Start taking your dog out as soon as your veterinarian gives you the go-ahead. Keep him on his leash, and bring along some plastic bags if he eliminates anywhere. Your first few trips should be short and positive so that your dog has a chance to learn about the world without being overwhelmed by it. Taking him with you on little errands to places such as the cleaners, bank, open shopping arcade, or the car wash lets him see new people, sights, and sounds. Outings are a boost to his confidence, especially when many people come up to admire him and ask to pet him.

If you have a puppy, it's a good idea to skip the dog parks for several months. They're not always the

*Use praise and treats to reward your dog for a job well done.*

*Well-socialized dogs are happy and secure.*

cleanest places, and he needs time to build up his immunity against disease. He'll encounter other dogs in a puppy kindergarten class or on walks through your neighborhood soon enough. These are great places for your Bichon to interact with other dogs.

You can always tell those dogs who are well socialized early in life. They're happy and secure and are a joy to be around.

## Crate Training

Rather than a jail, think of a crate as a doggy playpen. Whether you choose an open wire model or a solid-sided design, the crate is a safe haven where your dog can have his own downtime. Add a blanket, some favorite chews, and a stuffed toy, and your Bichon will look forward to hanging out in his own room.

A crate is invaluable during housetraining, traveling, or whenever you can't keep an eye on your dog. There, you can rest assured that he's safe and not getting into any trouble.

## How to Crate Train Your Bichon

Have the crate ready the day you bring your dog home so that he can become accustomed to it right away. He will

## Treats, Glorious Treats

You like receiving a paycheck, don't you? Your dog appreciates a reward for a job well done, too—but his payoff is food. To motivate your Bichon to perform the behavior you want, give him treats different from what he normally receives. Healthy human food, such as bite-sized bits of hot dogs, cooked chicken, turkey, apples, cheese, and roast beef, is especially enticing.

Being Good

## Reading Your Bichon's Body Language

In addition to barking and whining, dogs use their facial expressions and body positions to speak volumes to you. Learn this language, and you'll be able to understand what your Bichon is thinking. When your dog crouches down with his rear in the air, he's ready to play. If his tail is down, he's sad. Ears back? He's feeling fearful. More than 100 different canine facial and body positions are possible, but you can decipher them by observing your dog closely.

74

need a few days or even a few weeks to adjust to the crate, so be patient. Begin by placing his blanket and a few familiar toys inside and opening the crate door. Put the crate in the room where you are, and let your dog sniff and walk around inside without closing the door.

To entice him to investigate his den, toss some treats inside the crate or put his food in there. After a few meals or treats inside, try closing the door for a few minutes. Continue training your Bichon to like his crate by putting him inside when he's ready for a nap. Tell him he's a good boy and stay close by. Chances are, he'll settle down and snooze.

Take your dog out as soon as he wakes up. If he puts up a fuss, only take him out when he's quiet.

Otherwise you'll be rewarding him for not staying inside the crate. Gradually lengthen the amount of time you leave your dog inside. How long can your Bichon stay in his crate? Puppies will need to eliminate about every two hours. Adult dogs can be crated no more than four hours. The crate is not a day care center, and your dog shouldn't stay there continuously for eight or nine hours during the day—at night while he's asleep is the only exception.

In the evening, put the crate in your bedroom, next to your bed. This way you can tell him to settle down if he fusses. You'll also be close by in case he has to go outside to eliminate. Always give your dog a treat when you put him in his crate. That way, he'll look forward to going inside.

### Housetraining

Convincing your Bichon to eliminate outside the house instead of inside can be a challenge. Some people even say that toy dogs are harder to housetrain than larger breeds, but that's often only the owners' fault. Their messes are so small that most owners don't mind cleaning them up and so consequently don't enforce a consistent housetraining routine. Also, Bichon puppies are so low to the ground that it's hard to tell if they're getting ready to squat down and eliminate or not.

To housetrain your Bichon as quickly as possible, set aside as much time as you can so that you can monitor your dog's bathroom needs. Being patient helps, too.

## How to Housetrain Your Bichon

Keeping to a schedule is the key to housetraining. It goes like this: First thing in the morning, take your Bichon out of his crate and directly outside. Stay in the same spot with him until he goes to the bathroom, then praise him. Take him in for breakfast, and as soon as he finishes his meal, take him outside to the same spot he used before. Wait until the mission is accomplished, then praise him.

Once you're back inside, limit his freedom to one or two rooms only. This makes it easy to watch him. After 20 minutes or so, he'll be ready to go to the bathroom again, so expect to see him turning in circles or sniffing the floor. Whisk him out again. This is the bathroom pattern. Your dog needs to go outside when he wakes from a nap, after he finishes a meal, and before he goes inside his crate for the night. If you're diligent about keeping to this schedule, your Bichon will be trained in no time.

## If Your Bichon Has an Accident

Rubbing your dog's nose in his mess or hitting him with a rolled-up newspaper is the wrong way to housetrain your dog. Besides being cruel, these punishments will only make your dog sneak off to eliminate where you can't see him.

If you do not actually see him eliminating in the house but find a bowel movement, simply pick it up and dispose of it. Say nothing to your dog. If you see him eliminating inside the house, quickly pick him up (even in midstream) and take him outside while saying "No." Praise him when he goes outside.

## Basic Obedience Commands

Many training methods can be used to teach your dog basic obedience.

*Keeping to a schedule—taking your Bichon out to eliminate at the same times each day—will help him succeed at housetraining.*

With Bichons, positive reinforcement using verbal praise, treats, toys, or petting is very effective.

Clicker training uses a small handheld noisemaker for effective training. When your dog performs the desired behavior, immediately press the clicker and give your dog a treat. The *click* sound instantly lets your Bichon know that he did well and that a treat is on the way. If your dog isn't food motivated, give him a favorite toy or pet him.

You don't have to use a clicker to train your dog; it's simply a tool to aid you in training. Verbal praise and an immediate reward can accomplish the same goal. For the best results, always have fun while using any training method. Vary your training sessions and treats, and add little challenges along the way so that your dog looks forward to training with you. You always want to be the most interesting thing in your dog's life.

The sit *is the foundation for all other things you will teach your dog.*

## Sit

The *sit* is the easiest and handiest command to teach your dog. When you tell your Bichon to sit, you are in control. If someone opens your front door unexpectedly, tell your dog to sit so that he won't run out of the house. When a visitor arrives and your Bichon wants to greet your guest, asking your dog to sit and stay prevents him from jumping up to say hello. The benefits of sitting are endless, and this behavior is the foundation for everything you teach your dog to do.

## *How to Teach* Sit

To teach your dog to sit, take him to a nonslippery surface, such as carpet, and show him a yummy treat or a toy. Say your dog's name and "Sit." Bring your hand holding the treat slightly above his head. When your Bichon looks up at the treat, move your hand toward his tail. He should back up into the sitting position. When he does, give him the treat immediately and tell him "Good boy!" Don't pet him or he might get up, and don't give him the treat if he isn't sitting.

Otherwise, you're rewarding him for the wrong behavior.

What happens if your dog doesn't sit? Hold the treat in one hand, and use your other to gently tuck him into a sitting position. Don't force him. What happens if your dog still doesn't sit? Ask someone to sit on the floor with your dog standing between her legs. Repeat holding the treat slightly over your dog's head, tell him "Sit," and walk toward him so that he backs right up into your assistant and sits. Praise your dog and immediately give him the treat.

## FAMILY-FRIENDLY TIP

### How to Involve Your Child in Training

With the right supervision, your Bichon and your child can become great buddies. To establish a good working relationship between the pair, always teach your dog what you want him to do. Once the dog is trained, instruct your child what commands to use with him. Stress the importance of saying them in a strong tone without yelling and always while you're around to supervise. Children should never be expected to train a dog by themselves.

## Stay

You'll be using the *stay* command with the *sit* and the *down* commands. When you tell your dog to stay, this means that he must remain in the same position until you tell him it's okay to move—not before.

### *How to Teach* Stay

Attach your dog's leash to his collar and tell him to sit at your left side. This is the *heel* position. Fold up the leash in your palm so that it takes up most of the slack, and hold it firmly in your left hand. Tell him "Stay," and take one tiny step forward. If your Bichon moves, place him back in the original *sit* position. Move back to your dog, wait a few seconds, and repeat. If your dog stays, praise him and pat him once on the head. Don't be too exuberant with your praise or your dog will pop up. At first, he only has to hold the stay for a few seconds. As the training progresses, you can increase the distance and time.

## Come

This command is the most important behavior you will ever teach your dog. A lifesaver if he ever escapes from the yard or starts running into the street, use it whenever you want your Bichon to come to you.

### *How to Teach* Come

To train your dog to respond to the *come* command, put about 1 cup (236.6 ml) of dry dog food pieces inside a metal container with a lid. Sit your dog in front of you. Say his name

Being Good

> *When your dog "heels," he should maintain that position no matter where you walk.*

and "Come," and shake the can so that the food rattles. Give him a piece of food. Your dog isn't coming to you because he's sitting right there, but you're teaching him that when you say the word "come," the container rattles and he gets a treat. Repeat several times and tell your dog that he's a good boy.

At another session, rattle the food can and call your dog's name; say "Come" when he is in the same room with you. Repeat this exercise a few more times, and progress to calling your dog to come to you from another room while you're shaking the can. Remember to make the exercise fun!

## Down

The *down* command is helpful if you need your dog to stay in one place for an extended period. For example, if you take your dog with you to meet a friend at an outdoor café, having the dog lie down on command comes in handy. He'll be able to relax while you enjoy the visit.

### *How to Teach* Down

Begin with your Bichon in a *sit* position. Grab a treat; place your treat hand near his nose so that he has a chance to sniff it, and move your hand directly to the ground in front of him. As he begins to lie down to follow the food, say "Down." When his body touches the floor, give him the treat.

## Heel (Walk Nicely on a Leash)

Nothing is more aggravating than taking your dog out for a walk and having him pull ahead on the leash or run circles around you. Teaching your dog to walk beside you without yanking at the leash is well worth the effort. Your Bichon should walk on your left side, with his neck and shoulder area next to your leg. When you tell him to heel, it means that he should maintain that position no matter where you walk.

### How to Teach Heel

Start by putting some treats into your right pocket or into a fanny pack around your waist. Clip your dog's leash onto his collar and tell him to sit on your left side. Hold the leash in your left hand and show your dog a treat in your right hand. Say your dog's name and say "Watch me." As soon as he looks up at you and the treat, say "Heel" and walk forward.

If he forges ahead, show him the treat and turn sharply in a different direction. Give your dog the treat when he isn't pulling the leash and looks up at you. Tell him he's a good dog!

While you're just getting started, you only need to walk a few steps before stopping and giving your dog a treat. As he catches on to what you're trying to teach him, reduce the number of treats you hand out. When you practice, walk a few steps and stop. Then walk a few more steps and stop again.

## Tricks

It's no wonder that the Bichon's ancestors were circus entertainers— they love nothing better than pleasing people and making everyone laugh. Teaching your dog a few tricks is easy, especially once he has learned the basic obedience commands. Some Bichon favorites are: *high five, roll over, fetch a facial tissue, play dead, find the keys, jump through my arms,* and *take a bow.*

Begin by teaching your dog basic obedience commands, because most

## SENIOR DOG TIP

### Training Techniques for the Older Dog

Don't believe the old adage "You can't teach an old dog new tricks." Dogs continue to learn as they age. Although they may not be as alert as they once were, senior Bichons are more willing to please you than they were in their younger years. You may need more patience, but the effort is worth it. You'll be sharpening your dog's thinking skills and giving him something fun to do. Use short training sessions, and always keep them positive.

Bichons respond best to positive reinforcement training methods that use treats or toys.

tricks begin with a *sit-stay*. Next, choose a trick to teach your dog, and break it down into small segments that lead up to the final outcome. Put treats in your pocket or in a fanny pack around your waist so that you can quickly reward your dog when he shows the slightest promise of accomplishment. He will learn faster if you praise him for a job well done and if you schedule short, frequent lessons rather than one or two long sessions. Also, if you have other dogs, put them in another room during the training so that your dog won't be distracted. Above all, make sure that all learning is fun!

To teach your dog to high five, for example, sit down on the floor so that you are at eye level with him and are not leaning over him. Offer him your palm and say "Shake" or whatever command you want to use. Gently lift the elbow of your dog's front leg off the ground just a few inches (cm). Slide your hand down to the paw and shake it. Praise and give him a treat. Repeat this a few times over a few different sessions.

When your dog puts his paw in your hand without waiting for the command, it's time to teach him to give you the other paw. Begin by sitting at his eye level and say "Other paw." Always reward your dog when he gives you the other paw. Repeat a few times.

The next step is to have your dog raise his paw as high as he can. Hold out your palm at his chin and say "Shake." Praise and reward him for reaching the higher level. When you say "Shake," you can say "Other paw" and he will switch. Reward him when he gives you the correct paw.

## Finding a Professional Trainer

If you've never enrolled in a dog training class before, consider signing up for one. Look for small class size and an experienced trainer. There are many ways to train a dog, and every trainer has a favorite method. Your Bichon will respond best to positive-reinforcement training that uses treats or toys to communicate the behavior you want him to learn. Punitive methods that only focus on what the dog does wrong are cruel and ineffective. Choose a trainer who uses techniques you like.

Ask your veterinarian, breeder, or rescue coordinator for the names of trainers they recommend. Word-of-mouth from people who own dogs is also a great resource. Another way to locate a trainer is to consult professional training organizations, such as the International Association of Canine Professionals (IACP) (www.dogpro.org), the Association of Pet Dog Trainers (APDT) (www.apdt.com), or the National Association of Dog Obedience Instructors (NADOI) (www.nadoi.org).

Regardless of how cute your Bichon may be, no one likes a yappy, annoying, out-of-control dog. Certainly you want your family, friends, and neighbors to admire and respect your dog, so train him to follow the rules and behave. Everyone will thank you!

# Chapter 7

# In the
# Doghouse

One look at your sweet Bichon and no one would ever guess that he's a jester in disguise. He's inquisitive and a bundle of fun, but sometimes his antics aren't so cute and he may be somewhat annoying. The creative Bichon will push the limits and try to get away with as much mischief as he can. Also, because he is an independent thinker, he can have a one-track mind when it comes to getting exactly what he wants, when he wants it.

Despite the best training methods, your Bichon may misbehave once in a while. To begin correcting his problem behaviors, figure out why your dog is doing them in the first place. Boredom, insufficient exercise or attention from you, or health problems could all be responsible. Once you have determined why your Bichon is doing what he's doing, follow the steps outlined in this chapter to remedy the problem.

## Barking

All dogs bark to express themselves, but some Bichons don't know when to stop talking. Whether yours is just having fun or trying to protect you from intruders, the neighbors won't appreciate the constant communication. Your job is to teach your dog that barking without a good reason isn't allowed.

### Solution

Teach your dog the word "quiet" by keeping some food treats handy the next time he starts barking. Between barks, say "quiet" and give him a treat. After a few times

he'll turn his attention to you, and he'll wait longer between barks. You also can acknowledge your dog when he barks by telling him "That's enough."

If barking at strangers walking in front of the house is a problem, close all the curtains so that he can't see out, or make sure that your dog can't see out the gate in the yard. What he can't see, he can't bark at.

## Chewing

All puppies need to chew, especially when they are teething. Bichon youngsters are no exception. Unfortunately, they don't always choose their own toys to chomp on. When new teeth are erupting, your possessions are very soothing on sore

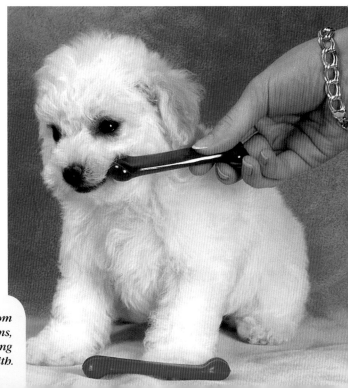

*To prevent your Bichon from chewing on inappropriate items, provide plenty of safe, interesting toys for him to play with.*

gums. Some pups are so determined to ease the discomfort in their mouths that they will gnaw on anything, including children's toys, chair legs, leather furniture, your purse and shoes, or even the floorboards. Adult Bichons will also chew the wrong things if they're bored. Just because your dog's jaw is small doesn't mean that he can't chew up big things with it!

## Solution

To prevent your Bichon from munching and crunching your prized possessions, keep them out of his sight. If something is on the floor or easy for him to reach, it's up for grabs and nibbles. Pick up items, and close off rooms or use a baby gate to keep your dog away from temptations you can't remove.

Supervise him at all times so that he doesn't have the opportunity to chew anything except his own toys. If you do find him chewing on something he's not supposed to have, offer him a small food treat as a trade. When he drops the item and goes for the tasty tidbit, tell him he's a good dog so that he thinks he's being rewarded for chewing something acceptable.

Provide plenty of safe, interesting toys, too, and rotate them every few days so that there's always something new for him to mouth and investigate. Small crunchy pieces of apples or

pears given between meals will keep his jaws occupied, too.

## Digging

Let's face it: Your little Bichon isn't going to cause a tremendous amount of damage to your yard if he digs. Then again, if you've just planted an expensive new shrub and your dog has dug it up, his small paws could ruin it.

Why would your dog want to destroy your property? It isn't intentional. Digging is actually a natural instinct for many dogs. A snug, warm hole in the ground is the ideal place to cuddle up in and soak up some rays.

On hot days, the earth also can be nice and cool, especially if it's beneath a tree. There are lots of interesting smells in the ground, such as beetles or mice a few inches (cm) down.

## Solution

If your Bichon is a digger, give him his own personal excavation site. Bury a few dog toys and treats in a designated location in your yard, and take him there. Tell him "Find your toy." Stay with him until he finds it so that he knows that this is the place you want him to dig in. Keep it interesting by burying different toys and treats so that he never knows what fun he'll find there.

Another way to deter your dog from digging up the landscape is to supervise him more closely when he goes out. As soon as you see those

front paws in motion, call your dog to you. When he comes, give him a treat or play ball with him. The goal is to be more interesting to your dog than the dirt is. It may take a few repetitions before your Bichon catches on, but the result is worth it.

## House Soiling

After your dog is trained, he may have a few inappropriate eliminations in the house. Accidents happen, but if he has too many, there may be a reason. Dogs don't suddenly forget everything they've learned. Maybe your Bichon wasn't as trained as you thought he was. Or if you've adopted him from a rescue or a shelter and were told that he was already housetrained, it's possible that he really wasn't. Perhaps he wasn't trained correctly to begin with, or he's spent most of his life in a crate or was confined indoors and doesn't know that he's supposed to go outside to eliminate.

Another reason for mishaps could be confusion or stress in his new surroundings. Dogs are very sensitive to changes in their environment, especially if there's a new addition to the family, such as a baby, an elderly relative, or a houseguest.

A medical problem can be responsible for house soiling as well, so have your veterinarian rule this out before beginning a training regimen. Bladder infections cause frequent urination, and diarrhea signals a stomach

*Your Bichon doesn't purposely want to destroy your garden— digging is simply a natural instinct for many dogs.*

# Finding the Lost Dog

Hopefully, your dog will never become separated from you, but if he does, begin looking for him right away. Don't assume that he will come back on his own because dogs can easily lose their sense of direction.

To improve the odds of finding your Bichon, follow these steps:

- Search every nook and cranny on your property. Bichons are small enough to fit into the tiniest spaces, so check behind your household appliances, under the family car or furniture, and inside drain pipes or crawl spaces. Try leaving some of your dirty clothes, such as sweaty gym socks, outside your door. It's possible that your dog will pick up your scent and find his way home.

- Walk through your neighborhood. Have all your family members call your dog's name. If he has a favorite squeaky toy, bring it along and squeak it. Tell everyone you see, including children, that you are looking for your lost Bichon, and hand out flyers with a description and picture of your dog and your phone number. Post multiple flyers within a 1-mile (1.6-km) radius of where your Bichon was lost.

- Place an ad in your local newspaper and offer a large reward. Money is a great motivator for returning a dog. Be sure to check the newspaper "found" ads every day, too, and try adding listings to local Internet websites.

- Call local veterinary offices and emergency clinics. Ask if any dog even remotely resembling your pet has been treated. If your dog was injured, someone may have taken him to a veterinarian or even a shelter or local rescue organization for treatment. Rescue organizations may be able to help you find your dog because they generally network with one another. Be sure to visit the animal control center and shelters every day or two because lost dogs are rescued all the time.

Above all, don't give up! Many dogs are found even weeks after they have wandered away from home.

upset or a more serious illness. Some medications have side effects that can include incontinence, too.

## Solution

Your job is to figure out what the problem is and go back to the basic housetraining lessons. This way, he

## SENIOR DOG TIP

### Older Dogs and Problem Behaviors

To train your older Bichon to stop an unacceptable behavior, you'll need time, patience, and some special food treats that he doesn't usually receive. You'll also have to be consistent. Reward him when he does something you approve of, such as sitting, lying down, or stopping barking. The next time he does this, add a word cue when he does the behavior, then reward him. For example, if your Bichon barks too much and at the wrong time, tell him "No bark" when he's quiet, then reward him with a yummy food treat. Repeat on cue whenever he's quiet. For house soiling, tell your dog "Good boy" when he urinates or defecates in the desired location outside, and reward him.

won't have a chance to make a mistake in the house.

If your Bichon is house soiling because he is confused or stressed in his new surroundings, give him a little extra attention and make a point of taking him outside more often to eliminate. Perhaps going for a walk in a new location will inspire him to empty his bladder more frequently outdoors.

To help your dog avoid house soiling, be consistent with housetraining methods, regardless of the weather or your schedule. Set designated times each day to take your Bichon out, and be sure to tell him what a good dog he is when the mission is accomplished outdoors.

Never reprimand your dog by screaming or hitting him, either with your hand or an object. Don't rub his nose in the mess, either, or take him over to the spot and shake or yell at him. These actions don't teach your dog anything, and besides, they're cruel.

You can only correct your dog's behavior while you see it happening— after the fact is too late. Interrupt him while he's urinating or defecating by telling him "No!" and picking him up and taking him outside right away. Be sure to praise him when he does urinate or defecate outdoors. By doing this, you are communicating to your Bichon that urinating and defecating isn't wrong; doing it inside is wrong.

Careful supervision and lots of patience work wonders when you're retraining your dog to eliminate outside. If you can't watch him, put him in his crate. Many dogs will not urinate where they sleep. If your Bichon is still eliminating in his crate, it's possible that the crate or exercise pen is too big. Use a smaller crate or pen. For retraining, your dog only needs enough space to turn around in.

## Jumping Up

Your Bichon has such light paws that you probably barely notice when he jumps up on you— until his paws are wet or muddy or he snags your suit! He doesn't know that he's just ruined your clothing because all he wants is your attention. Although it's hard to resist that cute little face looking up at you, picking him up just encourages him to keep leaping at you.

### Solution

To stop your dog from jumping up, only pet him when he's sitting or standing with all four paws on the ground. Don't touch him or even look his way when he's jumping up—that's the attention he wants. Teach him to sit (see Chapter 6) when he greets you, and reward him with a tasty food treat when he follows through. Be

*To help your dog avoid house soiling, set designated times each day to take him out to potty.*

consistent! If you pick him up one time and ignore him the next, he'll only launch himself at you even harder.

## Nipping

It's normal for puppies to put just about everything into their mouths, and that includes your hands. Unfortunately, puppy teeth are sharp, and they hurt when your Bichon nips at you. If this behavior isn't corrected while he's young, your dog will grow up thinking that this is acceptable play behavior. Even though your dog is probably not aggressive, and his biting may just be a game to him, he must learn that it's never acceptable for his teeth to meet human flesh.

Some Bichons think that it's fun to nip at your ear, hair, or clothing, especially if they're trying to get your attention. While this may look like a cute maneuver, grabbing at your hair hurts, and if you wear earrings, it can be dangerous. Your clothing can be ruined, too.

## Solution

To teach your Bichon not to nip at your hands, hair, or clothing, startle him by saying in a loud voice "Ouch, hurts!" the next time he reaches for you. Move away from him and redirect his thinking by quickly offering him one of his toys. Keep plenty of interesting chew toys around the house so that you can give him one at a moment's notice. Soon he'll reach for his own toys first when he feels the urge to gnaw.

If he goes back to his biting game, tell him "No bite," and end the session by putting him into his crate. Leave him there for 20 minutes and walk away. After a few times, he'll get the message that biting you is not a game he wants to keep playing.

## Separation Anxiety

Separation anxiety is probably the Bichon's biggest behavior issue. Bichons are very affectionate, and they bond quickly with their owners. Unfortunately, sometimes this close relationship becomes dysfunctional. If the owner leaves for just a few minutes, the dog may experience an overwhelming fear of being left alone and will become highly agitated. While the owner is away, the dog may pant, bark, whine, drool, run in circles, or pace to and from the window hoping to catch a glimpse of his beloved human once again. In the worst cases, a dog with separation anxiety may vomit, urinate, or defecate in the house. He also may become destructive and depressed, lick himself excessively, refuse food, howl, chew up household objects, and be destructive. Nothing seems to soothe a Bichon with separation anxiety until he sees his owner again.

Why do Bichons develop separation anxiety? Early neglect, poor socialization, and overly protective owners may be the culprit.

*A dog with separation anxiety may have an uncontrollable fear of being left alone.*

## Solution

To modify your dog's separation anxiety, try the following:

- Ask good friends or other family members to help with your Bichon's care. Ask them to feed your dog, take him for outings, and play with him when you're not around.

- Desensitize your dog to your absence. Leave him for a few minutes in his crate; return quickly, then reward him with a treat when he's quiet. Gradually build up the time you're away.

- Don't make a big fuss when leaving or returning to the house. Ignore your dog for 10 or 15 minutes when you return. This will help your dog accept your going and coming as just a normal part of the daily schedule.

- Vary your routine, so that your dog doesn't know what to expect. Leave the television on, pick up your keys without leaving, or move the car a few feet (m) without driving away from the house. This reduces his anxiety because he doesn't anticipate being left behind.

Curing your Bichon of separation anxiety will take time and patience, but you may be able to improve his behavior with the proper care. If none of these solutions ease your dog's condition, consult a canine behavior specialist or your veterinarian. Medications from your veterinarian are also available that may help.

Although no one was born a dog trainer, you can learn how to teach your Bichon to be the ideal companion. It just takes dedication, time, energy, and the belief that he is capable of learning anything you teach him to do. And just because your dog tries to "cute" his way out of behaving is no reason to let him get away with anything. Besides, training is the best way to show him you love him!

## FAMILY-FRIENDLY TIP

### Children and Bichon Safety

Your child may think that your cuddly Bichon is a live action figure, but he's really a fragile animal that can become injured easily. Even careful children can accidentally step on your dog and break one of his legs or cause serious injury if they drop him after picking him up. It's your job to protect your dog by teaching your child how to behave around your Bichon and vice versa. Always supervise, never allow the dog on the bed or couch where he can easily fall off and become injured, and put the kibosh on rough play. Never leave children alone with any dog, no matter how responsible your child may be.

# Chapter 8

# Stepping Out

Bichons love to party, and some party pretty hearty. They're intelligent and lively and enjoy getting out of the house and participating in a wide range of activities. To make sure that your Bichon stays healthy and safe whether he's on the road, in the air, or competing in a dog sport, be prepared. Take along all of the things that he needs, and give him the right kind of training.

## Travel and Vacationing

Part of the fun of having a petite, perky Bichon is being able to take him along with you wherever you go. Whether you're off on a short jaunt to the cleaners or a long drive or airline trip to a different city, this is an alert breed that enjoys a change of scenery every now and then. Just remember that, no matter where you go, your dog's health and safety come first. After all, he depends on you to keep him safe and happy.

### Travel Essentials

When going on a trip with your dog, don't leave home without these Bichon basics:

- bottled water or water from home
- chew toys
- close-fitting collar with identification tag
- crate
- dog bed
- dog food
- dog's identification tag with your address and phone number
- doggy booster seat or seat belt harness
- emergency and your regular veterinarian's phone numbers
- first-aid kit for your dog (include anti-diarrhea and allergy medication)

*No matter where you travel, remember that your Bichon's health and safety come first.*

- food and water bowls or disposable paper bowls
- grooming tools
- leash
- plastic bags for elimination cleanup
- prescription medication
- towels for wiping your dog clean
- treats
- waterless shampoo

**FAMILY-FRIENDLY TIP**

## Traveling with Your Dog and Child

What's a family vacation without the family Bichon? Just check before you leave home that your destination accepts children and dogs. Hopefully, it has both a safe kids' play area and a clean and roomy place to walk your dog.

To make sure that everyone has a good time, keep the travel schedule light and flexible, make frequent stops for bathroom breaks for both your dog and child, and allow plenty of time to rest.

Strangers are always attracted to a cute Bichon, so make sure that your dog is supervised at all times and never left alone.

## Travel by Car

When it comes to road trips, you'll need to take a few precautions. If your puppy or adult dog hasn't ridden in the car very much, it may take a few times for him to become accustomed to the new experience. Perhaps he'll be a little apprehensive or too exuberant in the car. Here's where some patience and training will come in handy.

Start by introducing him gradually to the world. Make sure that he's wearing a snug-fitting collar with an identification tag firmly attached—or have him microchipped—and be sure to take his leash, some bottled water or water from home, and a few plastic bags in case he needs to eliminate. To keep your dog safe while riding in the car, put him inside his crate and anchor it down, or use a doggy travel harness or doggy booster seat, which attaches to the seat belt.

Going somewhere on a hot day? If so, never leave your Bichon locked inside the car, even for a few minutes while you run inside the store or have a meal. The temperature inside the car can heat up to over 100°F (37.8°C) in just a few minutes. Leaving the windows partially rolled down won't help, either. This is too hot for a Bichon to withstand, and he'll quickly overheat and die.

Keep the first few trips short and happy, and don't feed your dog or let him drink a large amount of water one to two hours before you leave because some dogs get carsick. Once you're on the road, stop every three hours to give your Bichon a bathroom

*When traveling with your Bichon, don't leave home without his crate.*

ahead with the airline about its pet travel policies. There are strict travel rules regarding dogs on aircraft. While some airlines allow small dogs to be carried on in an airline-approved soft carrier and travel under the seat, others restrict them to riding in the cargo hold in a hard-sided crate. Either way, your dog will need a health certificate from your veterinarian 24 to 48 hours prior to departure, and the crate must be a specific size and have food and water bowls firmly attached.

A few airlines do not permit dogs under any circumstances.

## Accommodations

If you're planning to take your Bichon with you to a hotel or motel, call ahead and ask if dogs are permitted in guest rooms. Not every lodging welcomes dogs, although some will accept small ones. Arrange for your overnight stay well in advance, and expect to pay a small pet deposit when you check in.

When you check in, find out if there's a designated place to walk your dog, and clean up and dispose of any mess he leaves there. Before taking your dog inside the room, look under the bed and check the floor to make sure that no foreign objects are lying around that your dog might swallow.

Once inside, keep an eye on your dog at all times. If he accidentally goes to the bathroom on the rug, it's your responsibility to clean it up. You

break and the chance to walk around a little to stretch his legs. When you arrive at your destination, teach him to wait until you give the command that it's okay to get out of the car. You don't want him bolting out and running into traffic the minute the door is opened.

It may take a few tries to train your dog not to jump out of the car without your permission, but it's well worth the effort. Before you open the car door, tell your dog to stay. Slowly inch the door open, but if your dog gets up, give him the command again, place him in the *sit* position and close the door. If your dog remains seated as you slowly open the door, quietly give him a food treat and tell him "Good boy!"

### Travel by Air

If you're flying to another city and plan to take your dog with you, check don't want him chewing on hotel property, either. It's a shame that some irresponsible dog owners have forced many establishments to stop allowing dogs because of the damage they leave behind.

If you leave the room to go out, take your Bichon with you. Otherwise, he may bark and disturb other guests.

To locate pet-friendly accommodations, look online at sites such as www.petswelcome.com, as well as in automobile club and travel guidebooks.

## Sports and Activities

Bichons are active dogs who love to get out and have a good time. Today, many canine sports are available to keep you both busy. Some require training classes and practice sessions, while others aren't structured or competitive and are just plain fun. All extracurricular activities, however, require that you take a few precautions to keep your dog safe and healthy.

With every sport, start gradually and increase duration slowly. Hold off doing regimented jogging or agility that requires a lot of running with your Bichon until he's at least 18 months of age. His bones and muscles need time to develop and strengthen. The jarring before this age can cause permanent damage.

### Agility

This popular sport, which originated in England, has taken the canine world by storm. Agility is an obstacle course for both a dog and his handler. While the clock is running, dogs go through tunnels, scale an A-frame, straddle seesaws, weave through poles, and leap

*If you plan to travel with your Bichon on an extended trip, call ahead to see if dogs are permitted in hotel guest rooms.*

over hurdles, all under the direction of their handlers, who run around the course with them. Both speed and accuracy are important. Agility is fast and exciting, and Bichons just love it.

Several organizations sponsor agility competitions, including the American Kennel Club (AKC), the United Kennel Club (UKC), the United States Dog Agility Association (USDAA), and the North American Dog Agility Council (NADAC). Each offers several levels of competition and awards titles ranging from beginning to advanced. This precision sport takes time and patience for Bichons to master, but they don't mind because they love the workouts!

## Canine Good Citizen

Taking your Bichon to a basic obedience class teaches him a few manners that will always come in handy. After graduation, he can earn the American Kennel Club (AKC)'s Canine Good Citizen (CGC) certificate, which proves that he is well behaved and an asset to his community.

The CGC is a noncompetitive exam in which your dog will have to pass ten tests. These tests evaluate, among other things, his ability to

*Bichons enjoy agility, a sport that measures speed and accuracy over a timed obstacle course.*

accept a friendly stranger, walk on a loose leash, sit while being touched by a stranger, and remain calm in the presence of distracting sights or sounds.

For more information on the CGC program, contact the AKC.

## Conformation (Dog Shows)

In your eyes, the Bichon sitting on your lap is the most beautiful dog on the planet. Maybe he could even be a show dog! Showing your Bichon at dog shows is a fun way for you and your special canine to meet other Bichon owners and their dogs and to learn more about the breed.

At dog shows, an experienced judge evaluates how closely a dog meets the standard for his breed. Written by members of the national breed club and approved by the AKC, the standard is a lengthy description of how the breed should look, act, and gait (move). Qualities such as body structure and type, coat texture, head, tail, and temperament are evaluated. After a specified number of wins, the title of Champion (CH) is added before of your dog's registered name.

Dog shows were originally created to select the best breeding stock, and breeders use them today for the same purpose. Unlike car and appliance models that change over time, this is the best way that a breed can maintain its original appearance. Besides, dog shows are fun.

You need a show-quality dog to be competitive at shows, and if you

bought your dog from a breeder who actively shows her dogs, this person can help get you started in the sport. Contact the Bichon Frise Club of America (BFCA) for information about showing. Founded in 1964, the club encourages and promotes quality in the breeding of Bichons Frises. The breed was recognized by the AKC in 1972 and became eligible to compete in dog shows for Championship points a year later. All dogs are divided into groups according to the job they were originally bred to perform. The Bichon Frise belongs to the Non-Sporting Group.

In addition to watching a show on television, go to a few shows first without your dog (dogs must be entered in advance—even just to walk around) to see what shows are like. You'll have the opportunity to talk to Bichon exhibitors and learn what's involved.

## SENIOR DOG TIP

### Tips on Traveling with Senior Dogs

As Bichons age, their metabolism slows down, and they aren't as active as they once were. Senior dogs become set in their routines and are accustomed to their comfy pillows and favorite sun spots in the house. While he still needs some exercise and will enjoy getting out, don't count on your oldster to be an easy travel buddy, especially if he hasn't ridden in the car very much. A long car ride may be somewhat traumatic and physically difficult. If his sight and hearing are diminishing, he may become easily disoriented, so bring along his bedding and toys, which carry his scent and remind him of home.

Some elderly Bichons have occasional bathroom accidents, so you'll need to pack some clean-up supplies and a few towels and waterless shampoo to keep your dog clean.

If the prospect of showing your dog competitively appeals to you, begin by looking on the websites of the BFCA (www.bichon.org) and the AKC (www.akc.org). Both sites provide a wealth of information about Bichon behavior, care, health, history, training, and what a dog show is all about. You'll be able to find the Bichon breed standard on the BFCA website, plus pick up tips on how to groom your dog for competition. The AKC website explains the judging procedure and the rules governing the shows.

### Flyball

If your Bichon likes to play with a tennis ball, here's a fast and fun sport that's right up his alley. Dogs are organized into four teams, and they race on a relay system. They jump over four hurdles, release a ball from the flyball box, catch it in mid-air, and run with the ball back to the starting point so that the next dog can run his relay.

This is a team sport with a lot of camaraderie. To join a team, contact the North American Flyball Association (NAFA), which sponsors flyball competitions. Its website lists teams throughout the United and Canada.

### Freestyle

Combining obedience, dance, and music, this popular canine sport requires teamwork between you and your dog. You'll also need a costume for both of you. Freestyle takes practice, but once the music is on,

*Freestyle is a fun event in which a costumed dog and handler team dance to music.*

## Obedience Trials

In an obedience trial, a dog is scored on how well he performs a series of exercises, such as *heel*, *sit*, *lie down*, and *stay*. From this basic level to the advanced Utility level, which requires scent discrimination and directed jumping, Bichons are high achievers.

Dogs must be pre-entered for an obedience trial before they can compete. To be successful at these events, owners must take their dogs to training classes and practice between sessions.

Your dog can earn several titles through the AKC: Companion Dog (CD), Companion Dog Excellent (CDX), Utility Dog (UD), and Utility Dog Excellent (UDX). The UKC also offers the same titles.

## Therapy Work

Who can resist smiling when a Bichon enters the room? For hospital patients especially, receiving a visit from a happy little white dog works wonders in the cheer-up department. Taking your dog to greet children and seniors is a great outlet for a Bichon's good nature. These dogs love greeting people and are small enough to sit on a patient's

your Bichon will be ready to rock out. You'll be scored on enthusiasm, degree of difficulty of the movements, and musical interpretation.

The Canine Freestyle Federation Inc. (CFF) and the World Canine Freestyle Organization, Inc. (WCFO) sponsor freestyle events.

## Sports and Safety

Before getting your dog involved in sports, he should have a complete veterinary checkup, and all his vaccinations should be up to date. Your veterinarian may recommend that your Bichon be immunized against the highly contagious parainfluenza virus or the Bordetella bacteria before he begins meeting other dogs.

Another way to keep your dog healthy is to avoid taking him jogging or walking when the weather is hot. Too much sun exposure can cause fatal heatstroke. And if you're participating in competitive canine sports, your dog may have to wait his turn to compete, so you'll need to keep him cool in the shade. Take along a canopy tent or an exercise pen with a shade cloth so that your dog has a cool, comfortable place to hang out between events. Ice packs, extra water, and a first-aid kit are a must.

To keep your Bichon's feet from slipping when he's running, clip the hair short around his feet and footpads, and trim his toenails once a week. Whenever your dog is active outdoors, be on the lookout if he starts limping or seems to be in pain while on the move. Any exercise, including a lot of walking done on concrete or asphalt surfaces, can be hard on your Bichon's tender legs and feet. Check to see if your dog's footpads have abrasions or any red, swollen areas. Foxtail grass seeds, thorns, or bits of rock can easily become embedded on the bottom of his feet or between his toes.

lap, whether in a wheelchair or on the bed.

A few national programs, such as the Delta Society and Therapy Dogs International (TDI), register therapy dogs, and many communities have canine therapy programs that you can join. Most facilities require dogs to belong to a group and have a CGC certificate before they can participate.

## Walking and Hiking

In addition to providing healthy exercise for your dog, clipping on his leash and taking him for a walk is a great way to liven up his day. Just be sure to take him out while it's cool, and build up walk time gradually. Wait at least an hour after your dog has eaten, and stay away from busy traffic.

Your Bichon will enjoy going on short, easy hikes with you when the weather is cool and comfortable. But be prepared for a major grooming session when you get home. Dust, dirt, and other natural debris from the trail will stick to your dog's coat and will need to be combed and brushed out.

Few people can resist having fun with a Bichon. It's one of the reasons why you got one in the first place. He loves life and wants nothing more than just to please you. Active and intelligent, this breed deserves to have his mind challenged. Teach him gently, but teach him!

103

# Resources

## Associations and Organizations

### Breed Clubs
**American Kennel Club (AKC)**
5580 Centerview Drive
Raleigh, NC 27606
Telephone: (919) 233-9767
Fax: (919) 233-3627
E-mail: info@akc.org
www.akc.org

**Canadian Kennel Club (CKC)**
89 Skyway Avenue, Suite 100
Etobicoke, Ontario M9W 6R4
Telephone: (416) 675-5511
Fax: (416) 675-6506
E-mail: information@ckc.ca
www.ckc.ca

**Federation Cynologique
Internationale (FCI)**
Secretariat General de la FCI
Place Albert 1er, 13
B – 6530 Thuin
Belqique
www.fci.be

**The Kennel Club**
1 Clarges Street
London
W1J 8AB
Telephone: 0870 606 6750
Fax: 0207 518 1058
www.the-kennel-club.org.uk

**United Kennel Club (UKC)**
100 E. Kilgore Road
Kalamazoo, MI 49002-5584
Telephone: (269) 343-9020
Fax: (269) 343-7037
E-mail: pbickell@ukcdogs.com
www.ukcdogs.com

### Pet Sitters
**National Association of
Professional Pet Sitters**
15000 Commerce Parkway, Suite C
Mt. Laurel, New Jersey 08054
Telephone: (856) 439-0324
Fax: (856) 439-0525
E-mail: napps@ahint.com
www.petsitters.org

**Pet Sitters International**
201 East King Street
King, NC 27021-9161
Telephone: (336) 983-9222
Fax: (336) 983-5266
E-mail: info@petsit.com
www.petsit.com

### Rescue Organizations and Animal Welfare Groups
**American Humane Association
(AHA)**
63 Inverness Drive East
Englewood, CO 80112
Telephone: (303) 792-9900
Fax: 792-5333
www.americanhumane.org

**American Society for the Prevention of Cruelty to Animals (ASPCA)**
424 E. 92$^{nd}$ Street
New York, NY 10128-6804
Telephone: (212) 876-7700
www.aspca.org

**Royal Society for the Prevention of Cruelty to Animals (RSPCA)**
Telephone: 0870 3335 999
Fax: 0870 7530 284
www.rspca.org.uk

**The Humane Society of the United States (HSUS)**
2100 L Street, NW
Washington DC 20037
Telephone: (202) 452-1100
www.hsus.org

## Sports
**Canine Freestyle Federation, Inc.**
Secretary: Brandy Clymire
E-Mail: secretary@canine-freestyle.org
www.canine-freestyle.org

**International Agility Link (IAL)**
Global Administrator: Steve Drinkwater
E-mail: yunde@powerup.au
www.agilityclick.com/~ial

**North American Dog Agility Council**
11522 South Hwy 3
Cataldo, ID 83810
www.nadac.com

**North American Flyball Association**
www.flyball.org
1400 West Devon Avenue #512
Chicago, IL 6066
800-318-6312

**United States Dog Agility Association**
P.O. Box 850955
Richardson, TX 75085-0955
Telephone: (972) 487-2200
www.usdaa.com

**World Canine Freestyle Organization**
P.O. Box 350122
Brooklyn, NY 11235-2525
Telephone: (718) 332-8336
www.worldcaninefreestyle.org

## Therapy
**Delta Society**
875 124$^{th}$ Ave NE, Suite 101
Bellevue, WA 98005
Telephone: (425) 226-7357
Fax: (425) 235-1076
E-mail: info@deltasociety.org
www.deltasociety.org

**Therapy Dogs Incorporated**
PO Box 5868
Cheyenne, WY 82003
Telephone: (877) 843-7364
E-mail: therdog@sisna.com
www.therapydogs.com

**Therapy Dogs International (TDI)**
88 Bartley Road
Flanders, NJ 07836
Telephone: (973) 252-9800
Fax: (973) 252-7171
E-mail: tdi@gti.net
www.tdi-dog.org

## Training

### Association of Pet Dog Trainers (APDT)

150 Executive Center Drive Box 35
Greenville, SC 29615
Telephone: (800) PET-DOGS
Fax: (864) 331-0767
E-mail: information@apdt.com
www.apdt.com

### National Association of Dog Obedience Instructors (NADOI)

PMB 369
729 Grapevine Hwy.
Hurst, TX 76054-2085
www.nadoi.org

## Veterinary and Health Resources

### Academy of Veterinary Homeopathy (AVH)

P.O. Box 9280
Wilmington, DE 19809
Telephone: (866) 652-1590
Fax: (866) 652-1590
E-mail: office@TheAVH.org
www.theavh.org

### American Academy of Veterinary Acupuncture (AAVA)

100 Roscommon Drive, Suite 320
Middletown, CT 06457
Telephone: (860) 635-6300
Fax: (860) 635-6400
E-mail: office@aava.org
www.aava.org

### American Animal Hospital Association (AAHA)

P.O. Box 150899
Denver, CO 80215-0899
Telephone: (303) 986-2800
Fax: (303) 986-1700
E-mail: info@aahanet.org
www.aahanet.org/index.cfm

### American College of Veterinary Internal Medicine (ACVIM)

1997 Wadsworth Blvd., Suite A
Lakewood, CO 80214-5293
Telephone: (800) 245-9081
Fax: (303) 231-0880
Email: ACVIM@ACVIM.org
www.acvim.org

### American College of Veterinary Ophthalmologists (ACVO)

P.O. Box 1311
Meridian, Idaho 83860
Telephone: (208) 466-7624
Fax: (208) 466-7693
E-mail: office@acvo.com
www.acvo.com

### American Holistic Veterinary Medical Association (AHVMA)

2218 Old Emmorton Road
Bel Air, MD 21015
Telephone: (410) 569-0795
Fax: (410) 569-2346
E-mail: office@ahvma.org
www.ahvma.org

**American Veterinary Medical Association (AVMA)**

1931 North Meacham Road – Suite 100
Schaumburg, IL 60173
Telephone: (847) 925-8070
Fax: (847) 925-1329
E-mail: avmainfo@avma.org
www.avma.org

**ASPCA Animal Poison Control Center**

1717 South Philo Road, Suite 36
Urbana, IL 61802
Telephone: (888) 426-4435
www.aspca.org

**British Veterinary Association (BVA)**

7 Mansfield Street
London
W1G 9NQ
Telephone: 020 7636 6541
Fax: 020 7436 2970
E-mail: bvahq@bva.co.uk
www.bva.co.uk

**Canine Eye Registration Foundation (CERF)**

VMDB/CERF
1248 Lynn Hall
625 Harrison St.
Purdue University
West Lafayette, IN 47907-2026
Telephone: (765) 494-8179
E-mail: CERF@vmbd.org
www.vmdb.org

**Orthopedic Foundation for Animals (OFA)**

2300 NE Nifong Blvd
Columbus, Missouri 65201-3856
Telephone: (573) 442-0418
Fax: (573) 875-5073
Email: ofa@offa.org
www.offa.org

## Publications

### Books

Anderson, Teoti. *The Super Simple Guide to Housetraining*. Neptune City: TFH Publications, 2004.

Grant, Lexiann. *The Bichon Frise*. Neptune City: TFH Publications, 2006.

Morgan, Diane. *Good Dogkeeping*. Neptune City: TFH Publications, 2005.

### Magazines

**AKC *Family Dog***
American Kennel Club
260 Madison Avenue
New York, NY 10016
Telephone: (800) 490-5675
E-mail: familydog@akc.org
www.akc.org/pubs/familydog

**AKC *Gazette***
American Kennel Club
260 Madison Avenue
New York, NY 10016
Telephone: (800) 533-7323
E-mail: gazette@akc.org
www.akc.org/pubs/gazette

Resources

# Index

Note: **Boldfaced** numbers indicate illustrations.

Index

Index

## Acknowledgments

Special thanks to the Bichon Frise Club of America and to Stephanie Fornino for her support and professional expertise.

## About the Author

**Elaine Waldorf Gewirtz** writes about human and canine behavior, care, and health. The author of books and articles, Elaine is a multiple recipient of the prestigious Maxwell Award from the Dog Writers' Association of America and the ASPCA Humane Issues Award. A lifelong dog owner, she and her husband Steve live in Westlake Village, California, with their four-footed best friends.

## Photo Credits

james balzano, jr. (Shutterstock): 66
Chris Bence (Shutterstock): 33, 37
diane critelli (Shutterstock): 4, 14
Tad Denson (Shutterstock): 102, front cover photo
Karyn L. Giss: 112 (author photo)
Jostein Hauge (Shutterstock): 64
michael ledray (Shutterstock): 8, 39, 70, 82, 97, back cover (top)
Patricia K. McGuire (Shutterstock): 69
Photomediacom (Shutterstock): 101
stephen rudolph (Shutterstock): 94
April Turner (Shutterstock): 29
All other photos courtesy of Isabelle Francais and T.F.H. archives.

### REACH OUT. ACT. RESPOND.

Go to AnimalPlanet.com/ROAR and find out how you can be a voice for animals everywhere!